ONLY
SON

ONLY SON

JOHN JOHNSON

WITH JEFF COPLON

WARNER BOOKS

An AOL Time Warner Company

Warner Books, Inc., 1271 Avenue of the Americas, New York, NY 10020

Visit our Web site at www.twbookmark.com.

 An AOL Time Warner Company

Printed in the United States of America
First Printing: June 2002
10 9 8 7 6 5 4 3 2 1

ISBN: 0-446-52552-9
LCCN: 2002101076

Book design by Giorgetta Bell McRee

For my parents

Prologue

WHEN I WORKED IN TELEVISION FOR WNBC, THE NETWORK'S flagship station in New York, they used me all over the clock. In addition to anchoring the news at noon, my normal slot, I could be called in as early as 5:00 A.M. to sub on the morning show. The next day I might pop up on the evening or nightly news, or chase a story in the field through the afternoon.

I was paid handsomely for my labors. In the fall of 1996, I'd signed a four-year contract starting at more than half a million dollars a year. Management treated me well. I wore sleek Italian suits, wined and dined with the city's elite. I was living *la vida loca.*

My problem was my father, in a nursing home out on Long Island. Although I managed to see him once or twice a week, I felt perpetually neglectful and anxious. I made sure that the people at East Neck Nursing Center had all my numbers: home, work, cell. In an emergency, they were simply to call and I'd come. I left work early more than once when my father had bronchitis or pneumonia. If my boss seemed peeved, I ignored him.

The arrangement broke down in the summer of 1997. They'd rushed my father to the hospital and needed my signature to authorize a tracheotomy. When the call came, I was down in makeup for a tease for the noon show—not the news itself, but a pre-show promotion. I didn't get word until after my newscast, an hour later, because someone had decided not to "disturb" me.

Hey, better get John—his dad is dying!

Hold on, he's doing a promo!

Though the tracheotomy wasn't needed that day, the incident slung me over the edge. Frayed and exhausted, I'd soon recall the old joke, that it's always darkest before it turns pitch black. In August the doctor ushered me into his office and held an X-ray to the light. I could see the shadow on my father's left lung before he pointed to it: the shadow of death.

The doctor said, "This is very bad. It's indicative of a carcinoma."

I said, "How long?"

"A month, maybe two."

I received the news evenly. My father was eighty-two years old, and he'd spent most of them smoking two or three packs of Camels a day. Of late he'd looked so brittle that I'd sensed it was his time to die.

"Hey, Johnny boy," he said from the hospital bed. He feebly lifted his hand for me to hold.

"How you doing, Daddy-o?" I said, planting a ritual kiss on his forehead. He nodded and smiled, and said he was tired. I didn't stay long.

The following afternoon, I took a break from work at the old RCA Building. In the lobby, where my father once toiled as a janitor, I passed my photo in an illuminated display case, "The WNBC Experience." I went out into Rockefeller Plaza and found a bench near the skating rink, now ringed with the summer lunch trade. I gazed at the statute of golden Prometheus, which my dad once shined to a fare-thee-well.

In one generation I had made quite a leap, and what

did I have to show for it? One Ferrari, three ex-wives, four children, eight Emmys, and any number of prominent friends—"the whole catastrophe," as Zorba put it. Here I sat, a quasi-famous anchor guy at the number-one station in the capital of the world, and on my good days I felt jaded, and on my bad days . . .

At that moment, Lauren Hutton walked by. She flashed me her brilliant, gap-toothed smile in passing; she seemed to remember me from an interview. It is truly life-affirming to be acknowledged by a beautiful woman, but seconds later I was back to zero. That was when I knew it was over—when I saw that nothing stayed with me, not even Lauren Hutton.

I looked back at the statue and recalled the first time I'd seen it, as a nine-year-old holding fast to his hero's hand. Our trip to Radio City was half a century old, yet I remembered it more vividly than my last five vacations. I was a contemplative little boy. When I'd stood with my father at this spot and took in the view, I took it in completely.

But by high school I had no time for idle pleasure. I was too busy getting on with it, getting *out*. I wanted nothing like my father's life because his life had made him hateful, and I wanted to be nothing like him.

Since then I'd skimmed along like a surfer, mistaking speed for direction. I'd feigned to be pressing forward when I was really running away. These days I was running still, using my dense schedule to limit visits to the home. My father made me uncomfortable. When our conversation petered, there was nothing to connect us but a past of fear and pain. We were knit by a history too hurtful to revisit.

A few days after scanning the fateful X-rays, as I sat in stalled traffic on the George Washington Bridge, I realized that no one could give me permission to see my dad. I owned that permission; I simply had to seize it.

Three years before, I had squeezed my mother's dying into my glamorous career. By the time I crossed the Hudson River, I'd resolved it would be different this time. He might lie beyond love or redemption, but he was also *my father.* If I were ever to have a decent life, I'd have to do right by him now.

It was time to stop running. I was fifty-nine years old, and my father's death was imminent, and it struck me that I didn't know him very well. I had a few precious weeks to decode this difficult man—and, by extension, myself. Once the chain was broken, my chance would be gone. I could only hope that it was not too late already.

And so I excused myself.

CHAPTER ONE

WHEN THEY MET, SHE WAS A CHILD BEDAZZLED.

My mother was thirteen, brimming with a summer morning and its possibilities. She'd strapped on her roller skates, the vogue for young people in 1932, because skates were cheap and the streets were free.

She was a rangy girl, lithe and athletic. She found her rhythm along Edgecombe Avenue, in the Sugar Hill section of Harlem. She had to notice when a tall boy slid past her on the asphalt, then hurled himself into reverse, to skate backward as though it were the most natural thing in the world.

Giddy with speed, the boy was surely smiling as he passed her the second time. He was sixteen, old enough to know when he'd created a stir.

"Your father could skate backward as fast as he did forward," my mother would recall, a story I never tired of hearing. "Your father was really something."

It was plain that she loved him from the start.

Irene Young, my grandmother, grew up among farm people near Augusta, Georgia. (Andrew Young, the congressman and civil rights leader, came from another branch of the family tree.) She married a man named Marion Joseph Tutt, known to all by his simple last name, and gave birth to twin girls: my mother, also named Irene, and her sister, Marian. Times were hard; jobs were scarce for black folk. In 1921, when their daughters turned three, Tutt convinced Irene to chase a better life up North.

In Harlem, times turned harder still. Tutt never stopped chasing. A few months after they'd arrived, he failed to show for dinner one night, bound for parts unknown. He left Irene his name and little else. With no family to fall back upon, she and the girls fell destitute. They were put out from their apartment, thrown into the street with their sad down-home belongings for all the neighbors to see, until someone showed pity and took them in.

Fortunately for this story, Irene wasn't the type to roll over and die. Strong and square-shouldered, she took in laundry and cleaned houses and kept her daughters afloat. They might be uprooted and deserted, and go hungry from time to time, but Mama Tutt was a proud woman with a riotous sense of humor. She never lost her survivor's confidence.

It was tougher for my mother. I believe that she never got over that day on the sidewalk with the family's chipped dishes and rickety chairs piled about her. I think the little girl cracked that day. I think she felt touched by oblivion.

How could she be something when she had nothing?

Mama Tutt found cheap lodging over a Chinese restaurant in Hell's Kitchen, and my mother's earliest memory is of playing with poor white and Chinese kids. The Tutts and Youngs had a jumbled genealogy, from European to Choctaw Indian. With their freckles and "good" hair, the twins might have passed for white if you didn't know their brown-skinned mother.

But when they moved back to Harlem, the girls had it hard. Ostracized for looking different, they drew closer together, even gave names to each other. Marian, more se-rious and self-contained, was Sister, or "Sistah" in the Deep South inflection. My mother, the outgoing, effer-vescent one, became "Fatty"—though not fat in the least, she was much larger than Marian, who was tiny. When-ever Sister got picked on, Fatty fought for both of them.

Judging from her girlhood photographs, my mother was a sweet, demure-looking child. But she must have been tougher than she looked, just to get by. Just to grow up.

My paternal grandparents moved to New York from southwestern Virginia. George Johnson, a brawny laborer who could not read or write, was recruited as a strike-breaker. A rough-and-tumble man who bragged about drinking with Jack Johnson, the first black heavyweight champion of the world, he was quick with his fists in his own right. My grandmother Olivia, by contrast, was a model of gentility, a handsome, austere woman who worked as a maid but found her niche in the choir at St. James Baptist Church.

My father, John E. Johnson, was born in Harlem in 1915. He was the youngest of three brothers and easily the darkest, a stigma he bore bitterly. (His nickname was Jackie, but he also answered to Black Jack, even in his own family.) He had one desirable feature: straight hair. Olivia left it down to his shoulders until he was five or six, and dressed him like Little Lord Fauntleroy. He was fair game for every shabby street kid for blocks around.

Young Jackie admired his father's toughness and quailed at his cruelty. George Johnson bought him a Ger-man shepherd, an ideal pet, much loved. Then George came home late one night and carried Rex off; he'd lost the animal in a bar bet. My father was ten years old. When he cried, his father beat him.

After years on the docks and driving a cab, George saved enough money to buy a beauty parlor. Olivia worked on the ladies, while my dad kept the books. They were cobbling together a decent life—until disaster struck. My grandfather, then in his mid-fifties, jumped into a brawl with three men and took a frightful beating. My father had to collect him at the tavern and help him stagger home.

George Johnson never healed, and died of a stroke a few months later.

The family lost the beauty parlor; Olivia returned to work as a domestic. The oldest son, Manzie, flew off to be a jazz drummer. The middle son, Archie, had died young. My father was the smart one, the steady one. Now, at fifteen, his life as he knew it was over. The world crashed down on him.

A year later, when he met my mother, and then Marian and Mama Tutt, he thought they were the poorest people he'd ever seen. As low as the Johnsons had sunk, he was still better off.

My father somehow finished George Washington High School while working to support himself. A few months before commencement, Olivia took up with a man. When my father declared that he couldn't abide the boyfriend, his mother made a quick choice: "Why don't you leave, then?" So he left.

Black Jack's anger, as I see it now, was driven into him. If he was mean as a scorpion, he was made mean. He'd been kicked around every which way.

In 1936, Irene and Marian Tutt graduated from Wadleigh High School, both with honors. The next year, with Olivia springing for a two-dollar wedding dress, my mother married my father at St. James. She was nineteen, he was twenty-two. They had a little party afterward at Olivia's flat, which they'd been sharing (after the boyfriend cut and ran) for lack of any other place to stay.

Over the decades to follow, I'd wonder what my mother had seen in her dour sweetheart. But I wasn't seeing him through her young eyes. Jackie Johnson was an inch over six feet tall, with broad shoulders and a tight waist, a worthy partner for swingin' at the Savoy. He had long, smooth, beautiful hands, with a pianist's tapered fingers. He was bright and well-spoken. To my mother, who said *earl* for *oil,* he sounded positively refined.

In fact, the newlyweds had much in common. Both were fatherless, both had domineering mothers. And they both were damaged characters, formed by eviction and abandonment. The one became needy, dreamy, insecure, and vulnerable, quick to hold to any reed within her grasp; the other angry, twisted, insecure, and jealous, with a hard contempt for women.

They would cling together for the next fifty-eight years.

They moved into a basement apartment on Edgecombe Avenue, not far from where they'd met. My mother was soon pregnant. While my father worked odd jobs and drove a cab at all hours to make ends meet, his bride took charge of my prenatal education. Hewing to a curriculum out of some magazine, she listened to Bach, Mozart, Beethoven, Chopin; she trekked to the Metropolitan Museum of Art.

I was born on June 20, 1938, in the free public ward at Harlem Hospital. Due to an outbreak of bed fever, my mother and I were quarantined for ten days, barred from all visitors. From the beginning we were a party of two, with my father set apart. Still, he must have thrilled to the news of his strapping son, nearly eight pounds at birth. The certificate read: John E. Johnson Jr.

His name was my name, too.

"First day he came home he smiled and showed his dimple on his right cheek," according to a log my mother kept. "He smiled continuously. No one believed us when we told them how Johnny smiled." She went on to record

my first-year milestones: a cold at one month ("We became alarmed and called for the doctor, but he soon
calmed us and told us it was very slight"); my first rattle,
promptly broken; my first words, at six months: "Da da."

To my mother, dirt was the enemy. A ruthless cleaner of
her gloomy little flat, she now faced the ultimate challenge: a baby. Like many hapless firstborns, I was scrubbed
and pressed and starched till I yelped in pain. Please believe that I never had a spot of diaper rash; I was laundered
a dozen times a day. Add my father's faith in cod liver oil,
and I was pretty much spotless, inside and out.

Once I took to toddling, I was dubbed "Little Johnny
Boy." With a head too big for my body, I spent my early
childhood lurching forward, struggling not to tip over.
But fall I did, till it became a family slapstick joke.

To my mother I was a source of blushing pride. A
month shy of my second birthday, she listed twenty-
seven of my noteworthy achievements. A few examples:

1) *Talk in 3-word sentences;*
2) *Go up stairs without any help . . .*
7) *Could throw and play ball very well. Loves a
   ball . . .*
10) *Could imitate the oink of pig, the moo of cow . . .*
17) *Feed self very well without spilling a full cup of
    milk. Could eat with a fork very good . . .*
18) *Had 14 teeth and 2 coming in bottom, by the time
    he's 2 years old he will have 16 teeth . . .*
20) *Bladder control perfect—never wets himself . . .*
21) *Has never been constipated . . .*
24) *Plays with other children well, not selfish, very
    free-hearted . . .*

In 1941, lured by hopes of a federal paycheck, my father led us to Washington, D.C., where friends put us up
till we settled. I was three years old. Lodged on a spank-

ing new pullout sofa, I received a visit that first night from the Little Man, who was up to his old tricks.

It's okay, he said. (Our dialogue never varied.) *You're in the bathroom. You can go to the bathroom.*

And I cried, *No, no, no, I'm not in the bathroom!*

Sure you are, the Little Man said, and he conjured a sound of running water. *Go ahead, try it . . .*

And I said, *Gee, I* am *in the bathroom.* I relaxed, and then . . . *Oh no! No!* But it was too late. I heard the Little Man laughing and felt the dread warmth at my middle. From peeing in my dream, I awoke to wetting my bed. Again.

Soon enough came morning, and the grown-ups gathered 'round.

My father was angry: "Why didn't you go upstairs?"

My mother was upset and defensive: "He *never* wets the bed." Which made me indignant, because I knew it was a lie. I wet the bed all the time.

I remember standing there and thinking, *I'm so wet and cold, and everybody's mad at me. I wish somebody would dry me off.*

This is my oldest memory, my first consciousness of being *me:* a swell of choking humiliation.

We moved into a semi-attached brick house on Savannah Place, in a new black neighborhood called Anacostia Flats. A wooded backyard was ideal for exploring and my mother's sun-dried laundry. Our neighbors had government jobs and soon my father did, too, as a photostat clerk. Some even had cars.

It was the best living I'd ever have under my parents' roof, but it wasn't carefree. Though deathly afraid of the dark, I went to bed with my lamp off and my door shut, two of my father's many rules. My eyes clung to the pale yellow sliver from the hallway, the fine line between me and the void.

One night, not long after we'd moved, I woke up terrified and called for my mother. Ordinarily she'd rush in to comfort me. If my daddy consented, she might even leave my door ajar. But this time no one came.

It was very dark and I was alone. Inert. The moon shadows waxed more macabre by the minute. At last I got up my courage, crept to the door, and shoved it open, screaming, *Mama! Mama!*

No answer.

I ran out the lit hallway to my parents' bedroom: nobody there. I padded down to the living room: empty. I searched the whole house except for the cobwebbed basement, which scared me even when someone held my hand.

As frightened as I was, I kept my composure. I looked out the living room window, across the street to Johnny and Bill Pattersons', my parents' best friends. (Johnny drove a maroon-colored cab, and why they called his wife Bill was a mystery.) The lights in the house were blazing. *They must be there,* I thought.

Savannah Place buzzed with traffic, even at night. I'd have a cat run over on that street; a friend's little boy was killed there. But in my need for *Mama,* no danger could deter me. I went back upstairs, threw a coat on over my pajamas, found my shoes and a wool hat. I walked out into the dark and crossed the street to our neighbors'. It was noisy inside. I knocked as loud as I could.

When Johnny Patterson opened the door and looked down, everybody cracked up. They'd been partying for quite a while, I guess. Back home my mother reeled into the living room and slipped and fell on the floor. It was the first time I saw her drunk.

For as long as we lived in Washington, I'd never again trust my mother to stay put. Many were the nights that I'd hike myself up on the double bed beside her, to make sure she was there. Until my father objected and I had to go back to my scary cave, stepping lightly around the shadows just in case.

I was the runt on our block, the last to start kindergarten, the outsider. Worse yet, I looked delicate in my short pants, not to mention "perky" clean. Each day after school, a sturdy boy named Sonny led the neighborhood toughs in chasing me home. It was a long, long way to run. If Sonny caught me, he'd beat me up. If I escaped, the gang's jeers would trail me down the street: *Scaredy cat!*

One warm spring day I narrowly made it to my door, bawling as usual. I felt warmed by the sight of my mother behind the screen . . . but something was wrong. She wasn't her sympathetic self. She looked at me squarely and said, "You go on out there and fight that boy, or I'm not lettin' you in this house."

I could not believe it. My own mother turning me away in my need—such betrayal! I looked back across the street, where Sonny stood with his fists balled. I despised his scrinched-up face and its crown of tight ringlets; I despaired at how big and strong he looked. Sonny was in second grade, at least two years older than I (and maybe more if he'd been left back, which seemed likely). His arms were built for inflicting pain. On Savannah Place, Sonny was *the guy*. No way on God's earth I could beat him.

On the other hand, my mother had her mind made up, and I knew how unyielding she could be. If I didn't fight Sonny, she might never open the door. I might lose her forever. It was a Hobson's choice, all right, but I had no recourse.

Wailing my heart out, the sweat cold on my skin, I slowly marched across the street. I remember thinking, *Maybe if I take a swing and run, she'll let me back in.*

Or maybe Sonny would beat me to death.

Next to the bully stood Mickey Patterson, our neighbors' sloe-eyed daughter, the cutest girl on the block. It wasn't enough that I'd be taking a fall before my mother. I'd be licked in front of Mickey, my first crush.

Excited by the blood sport in the offing, Mickey began to singsong:

Johnny on the ocean,
Johnny on the sea,
Johnny broke a milk bottle,
Blame it on me.
I told Ma; she told Pa,
Johnny got a whipping,
So ha-ha-ha!

I think it was at Mickey's third chorus that I lost my mind. I strode up to Sonny, closed my eyes, and swung as hard as I could. I felt something give and heard him grunt, and I hurled myself into the righteous fury of the picked-upon. My little stick arms were a blur. I was pummeling Sonny helpless, until somebody pulled me off or he stumbled away, I can't remember which.

When my mother finally let me in, I was weeping with catharsis. She smiled at me and said, "That's my Johnny Boy." When my father came home from work, I gave him a blow-by-blow replay.

My world changed. I was unafraid, and hence invulnerable. None of the kids bothered me anymore. I began chasing Sonny home from school and punching him whenever I could. I might happily have beaten him every day for all time. Once I pushed him down some steps for fun, and he hurt his leg and gimped away puling.

Sonny's mother took exception and came calling with a few of her friends. Sizing up Irene Johnson as some "high-yella" pushover, they'd underrated her devotion to the child behind her skirt. It was a bad mistake, because they'd also misgauged her physicality.

My mother was five-foot-six and could run like a deer.

A few months earlier, she'd escorted my father to the bus stop for his ride downtown to work. As the bus rounded into view, he realized he'd forgotten his office keys. He told his wife to go get them—and off she ran through the yards in her dress and heels, hurdling picket fences in full stride, racing a long block and back before the bus left. It would be many years before I beat my mother sprinting.

Now she glared at the Sonny Protection Society and snarled, "You all get out of here, go on! Sonny started it."

When the women persisted, my mother barreled out at them. She chased them off our porch and clear across the street. Bill Patterson was shouting, "What's wrong with you, Irene? You're acting crazy!" All the neighbors were shocked. But I thought it was great. My mother might be passive with my father, but she was the scourge of Savannah Place. I could lick Sonny, and she could lick Sonny's mom! It was a new bond between us.

"Now listen," she told me, after the mob was routcd, "you shouldn't push him like that." I eased up on Sonny, who was too wary to retaliate. But I knew that my mother wasn't angry, because she couldn't stop laughing at how the worm had turned.

Garfield Elementary was a "separate but equal" school, which meant it was understaffed and altogether underwhelming. For lack of funding, we attended half-day sessions in a gray building with gray wood floors. The highlight of our year was the May Pole dance, which required endless rehearsal. Each child held the end of a crepe streamer tied to a pole in the playground. We walked in a circle—some clockwise, some counter-, dipping under one another as we passed—until the pole was swathed in multicolored crepe.

I thought the May Pole dance was dumber than dirt. The only thing more pointless, it seemed to me, was our annual lesson in horticulture. We learned how to plant radishes, which never sprouted worth a damn, and who'd want to eat the nasty things, anyway?

If the kindergarten curriculum was limited, my mother's expectations were anything but. In my spring term report card, she wrote, "We are happy to see that Johnny has improved in his work a great deal, and will do all in our power to see that he continues to do so."

In first grade I cut my knee on a nail. It became infected and grossly swollen, and laid me up for weeks. To keep me from falling behind, my mother bought a small chalkboard and drilled me in bed on my ABC's. She drew pictures to illustrate each letter: apple, bunny, corn on the cob . . . For H she drew a horse.

I was fascinated. The horse looked so real that it seemed to be moving, and I begged my mother not to erase it. She was wise enough to suspend the lesson and leave me to my new obsession.

I began by gently rubbing out part of the horse's head, then tracing over the ghost line that remained. I moved on to the mane and neck, the flank, and so on, erasing and retracing over and over again, with painstaking exactness, without a mote of boredom.

The next day I took the artist's leap. I bore down with the eraser until my mother's horse was gone. For a while I stared at the vacant black rectangle, hesitant and regretful. I picked up the chalk and began to draw, freehand, when something magical happened. I could still *see* the horse with my mind's eye. My hand flew over the board as though enchanted.

When I finished, flushed with the grace of making something from nothing, my mother agreed that my horse was every bit as fine as hers. Before bed she read to me from *Black Beauty*: a perfect day.

By second grade I'd lost all respect for my teachers, who were shrill and incompetent. My real teaching came at night, at home, where I learned to write in script two years early. At the chalkboard my jolly mother was a martinet, humorless and impatient. To stay on her good side, I worked hard and became a quick study. In school I was one of those annoying children whose hands strained heavenward, pleading to be called upon. My classmates called me Mr. Smartie, with less than starry admiration.

That year, to my chagrin, my mother became a substitute teacher at Garfield. I lived in horror of the days that she'd pop up in my classroom and hector me in public. My classmates would tell me, "We don't want your mother, 'cause she's strict. She makes us do work!" My mother had no license, no training, not a day of college, and she might have been the ablest teacher there.

We rarely left the neighborhood except on Saturday mornings, when my mother and I rose in the dark to venture downtown for our wartime rations. We set off at four in the morning to take a bus that went forever, then a trolley. I'd be sleepy, and frigid with cold in the wintertime, but we had to be on line with our ration book by six o'clock if we wanted a chicken and some eggs that week. I hated standing there because you could see them plucking the freshly slaughtered poultry in the next lot, and the smell was overpowering.

Downtown Washington was white Washington. I felt my mother's trepidation as she clutched my hand, absorbed her sense of not belonging. Though New York had its own de facto segregation, my parents weren't used to the South. My father griped that he'd lost promotions to ignorant white kids from outside the department, and that half of them were draft dodgers.

(For his own part, my father owned a deferment for his allergies, which seemed provoked by anything military. When he took me to a warplane exhibit, I couldn't wait to get a close look at the P-38, one of the fastest American fighters at the end of World War II. But no sooner did we enter the grounds than my dad fell into a spasmodic sneezing jag, and we had to leave.)

Thwarted on the job, he vented his frustrations at home. The worst fights came in the evening, triggered by my mother's drinking and my father's deranged jealousy. One night I heard a *crack* and ran downstairs to Bill Patterson haranguing, "What's wrong with you, Irene? You can't let nobody be hitting you."

The next morning her cheek was still pink. I knew something was wrong. I certainly didn't like the idea of my father hitting my mother. But I figured that married people behaved that way sometimes, like it or not.

I took my own discipline mostly in stride. When my mother spanked me for staying too late at hide-and-seek, or some other venial sin, it was easy to take. If she told my father what I'd done, she'd make clear that she'd already handled it. She tried to protect me, save for one unforgettable lapse.

The local tadpole pond lay strictly off-limits, as Mother worried that I'd drown. When my friends came by on their way to the pond one afternoon, I made up some story to get out of the house and join them.

I'd yet to unlace my shoes and try the muck before I heard my mom calling, "Johnny, *Johnny!*" She'd tracked me down; the game was up. I tried to slink off, but she wasn't fooled, and it was no use trying to outrun her. I had *lied to my mother,* and she was fuming. She broke a switch off a tree and spanked me up the street in front of all the kids.

Unfortunately for me, my father got home before my mother had time to cool off. She repeated what had happened, and regretted it, I'm sure, as the words left her mouth.

Lying was inexcusable in my father's book. He judged that I needed a second spanking. And with my father, a spanking was a beating.

He turned me over his knee and, oh, he hit me hard. I can still feel the sting of his big right hand through my pants. He kept on methodically hitting me—beyond tears, past any conceivable purpose. I remember his stale smoker's odor and how much I yearned to escape it.

If there was a particular moment when I began to dislike my father, that might have been the one.

In the postwar summer of 1946, when I was eight years old, I found pleasure in the simplest games. One day I made a contest out of running up and down a flight of steep outdoor steps to our basement.

My mother, out hanging the wash, eyed me and scolded, "Be careful going down those steps!" She had grounds for concern. Little Johnny Boy had pitched down the stairs indoors half a dozen times, headfirst, and only some lucky bounces had spared me a concussion.

Like any self-respecting boy, I ignored her. Two or three runs later, as I reached the top and turned to skip back down, I felt my balance slipping. I tried to grab myself—*Oh, no!*—but gravity won out.

As I caromed down the bare cement, it hurt so much that I thought I would probably die. When I hit bottom, I saw stars, then my mother gawking down at me, flailing her arms. Her mouth gaped in a silent scream; my hearing had clicked off. I saw the fear on her face, the wild look in her eyes, and I *knew* I was going to die. When I somehow stood up, it made matters worse. My mother bore the look of a person gone mad.

This is what undid her: a hole on the side of my forehead, pulsing blood.

My father, home for the weekend, ran to the scene and stood at my mother's side. Then everything went black. I wiped the front of my face, and my hand came away crimson. The blood was blocking my eyes.

I remember saying, "I'm dead," and I fainted.

*　　*　　*

To do his bit for the war effort, my father had enlisted as the neighborhood's air raid warden. He'd go out at night with a flashlight and the coolest hat I'd ever seen, a white metal helmet with his title in block letters. While the Japanese never got around to bombing Anacostia Flats, his vigilance paid off. He had taken a mandatory course in first aid, and now he'd have a chance to use it.

I revived on our front porch, my head cradled in my father's arms. He was doing what he'd been taught, applying pressure with gauze to stanch the bleeding. A ring of neighbors hovered over us, debating whether to rely on the ambulance. Somebody said, "He needs treatment and we don't know what we're doing. Let's wait for them."

Somebody else said, "He'll be dead by the time they get here, if they ever come." That threw my mother into fresh hysteria, and it didn't help my morale, either. I was fully conscious, but paralyzed. My head was one big throbbing pain, and the rest of my body seemed far away.

Johnny Patterson won the argument: "Fuck the ambulance, we'll take him in my cab." My father picked me up and held me in the front seat. As we raced away, my mother howled and reached out to me, but the neighbors held her back. My terror revived. I had never seen her so lost.

We dashed downtown. The jostling made me sick— that and the pain, which washed over me in waves. My father had blood all over him and I was startled by how red it was.

"Am I going to die, Dad?"

"No, Johnny, it's all right. You're going to be fine."

When we arrived at Unity Hospital, my father wasted no time; he'd been there once to patch a hernia, and knew the drill. As he carried me to the side of the huge building, he spoke in a low, urgent voice. He promised me all sorts of toys, including a P-38 with a double tail, my fantasy plane. He kept repeating that I'd be all right.

He was a great comfort, my father.

The emergency room was a zoo of distress, from open stab wounds to chicken pox, and not a gurney in sight. Everyone stood packed shoulder to shoulder, as in a stalled elevator to hell. My father burst in yelling, "This child needs help! *My son needs help!*" As the gauze ran out, he pressed my head with his bare hand. Whenever he shifted his hold, my blood spilled freely.

After too many minutes, a door swung open to reveal a man in a green uniform. "All right," he said. "Anybody who needs help, come on over here." As muddled as I was, I considered the doctor truly stupid. Why would anyone be here if not for help? But there was no triage in the colored emergency room at Unity Hospital. There was only a milling chaos, a Babel of moans.

Suddenly I found myself rising in the horizontal, high over the clustered bodies, till I nearly scraped the cracked plaster ceiling. My father, a tall man to begin with, had hoisted me above his head like a barbell, his right hand clamped to my injury. He raised me easily, with power in reserve. To myself I wondered, *Why is he lifting me up like this? So those people won't cough on me?* It seemed strange, but I felt a new safety.

My father would not fail me. He would not let his child die.

"Take my son!" he yelled. He muscled through the crowd until he faced the doctor. Still holding me aloft, my father appealed to him: "My son, he's only eight—he's *bad!*"

He made an impression. The doctor glanced up at my head and motioned for my father to follow him through the inner door. We found ourselves in a small examining room, where the first man greeted his partner.

I had not been inside a hospital before, nor ever spoken to a white person. Now two of them were roughly setting me on a cold steel slab. My father was ranting in his agitation, trying to explain what had happened, and one of the doctors said curtly, "We can see, you don't need to tell us."

I was afraid of these people. They didn't ask my name, or say hello or *anything.* I'd never met a grown-up who wouldn't say hello, and I reasoned that they didn't like me.

After cleansing my wound, one of them trained a light on my forehead. The other began sewing me up, using a tweezers to lift the flaps of my torn skin and pull them together. His arms were matted with dark hair. As I tracked the needle's journey, and the stabbing pain that followed, I began to squirm and cry.

"Hold him still!" the stitcher said, his last words to either one of us. My father leaned over to hold me down. He was very close and I could see that he was crying, too. The novelty distracted me, until I'd hushed enough to make out what he was saying:

Please don't cry, don't move. It only hurts for a little bit. I'll get you that P-38, I'll get you a Lone Ranger ring. You'll be okay, don't move, don't move . . .

The doctors chatted away. I couldn't understand what they were saying, but I knew it had nothing to do with me. The stitcher was smoking a cigarette. Midway through the procedure, a clump of ash dropped and wafted toward my head. I felt a stab of panic: *What if the ashes get in my eye?* There was a moment of confusion. The doctor paused while his colleague took the cigarette from his mouth, then went back to work.

I looked at my father, and the tears streaming down his cheeks, before I passed out one more time.

They released me without an X-ray or so much as a pill for pain. I woke that night at home, on my back on our living room couch. It hurt terribly where I'd been stitched, and the swelling lasted for ages. For days I could barely turn my head.

As I mended, I was filled with gratitude. For my kind nurse of a mother, of course, who carried me to the bathroom and salved my brow with cold compresses soaked in witch hazel. But even more for my father, who had saved my life. He'd done everything right in my crisis; he'd been a real father to me.

It hurt a lot more when he hit me after that.

I was still a downstairs invalid when I overheard my parents talking at the kitchen table. It was time to leave the South, my mother said. My father was about to be laid off, and my school wasn't getting any better. My injury was the last straw. My mother was appalled that the ambulance never did arrive that day. She could not rest easy after that.

"It's not worth it," she said. "At least in New York you can get some decent medical attention."

My father sat in full agreement. Never raised to know his place, he was too old to learn it now. The doctors at Unity Hospital left me with a faint lifelong scar, a two-inch diagonal running parallel to my right brow. But my father's mark ran longer and deeper. He would not forget how they sewed me up like a dog, or how they'd cut him down to size after he'd stood so strong and tall with me. He'd witnessed the most deflating thing a man can see: an image of himself helpless in his own son's eyes.

My parents could not remain in such a town, though they had friends and a good house there, and prospects for a better life. They resolved to move back to New York, back home, unsuspecting that the ride would be all downhill.

CHAPTER TWO

ST. NICHOLAS AVENUE TOLD A TALE OF TWO HARLEMS. DUKE Ellington lived on one side, in a grand masonry apartment house. Olivia Johnson lived on the other, in a railroad flat on the second floor of a dingy, shingled walk-up. To save money while my father searched for work, we moved in with her.

There were three rooms, including a kitchen off the entryway. My parents and I stayed in the middle chamber, my grandmother in the front. With only a curtained doorway between us, no one had much privacy.

Like my mother, Grandma Johnson would not tolerate the slightest disorder in her apartment, not a salt shaker out of place. But she couldn't erase the tenement smell, that stubborn blend of mildew, roach poison, and general decay. It was a constant reminder of our big step backward.

My dad's mom was prim and proper and a bit of a show-off. Mama Tutt called her "a little hinkty lady, struttin' around with her butt in the air like she was better than the rest of us." Grandma Johnson was a housecleaner, like Mama Tutt, but she cleaned for a better class of people, a white family downtown. Pedigree mattered to Olivia. She had little use for her up-from-Georgia daughter-in-law.

Though I liked Grandma Johnson, in spite of her airs, I held back out of loyalty to my mother. But when it came to my grandmother's cooking, my passion was unbridled. Her food was beyond the beyond, in the classic Virginia tradition: biscuits like cumulus clouds, smothered pork chops, the best apple pie, the best iced tea.

My favorite dish of all time was Grandma Johnson's Brunswick stew. She'd start with the lima beans, leaving them in water to puff up overnight. She'd add shucked corn and tomatoes, and spare ribs and chicken and a little bit of ham. She'd season it just right, with pepper and a bay leaf and a spoon of cane sugar to make the flavors sing.

I could happily have eaten Brunswick stew every night, and in quantities to amaze my grandmother's gentleman caller. Mr. Clark was a doorman and well turned out, and all stood in wonder at his appetite. As puny as I was, however, I could match him biscuit for biscuit. As I tucked into my third helping, Mr. Clark would exclaim, "Lord, that boy can eat. He sure can eat. You have to feed this boy, he really can *eat!*" He might cast a wistful glance when I gobbled the last piece of cornbread, but I believe that he admired me, like an aging champion who has glimpsed the future.

My Uncle Manzie, Grandma Johnson's prodigal son, lived in the apartment across the hall. He was eight years my father's senior, though you wouldn't know it from his boyish grin or his hep-cat lingo.

A palomino-colored man, Uncle Manzie wore his hair slicked back and had a pencil mustache like Cesar Romero's. He was built like my father, tall and slim, except for a barrel chest that belonged on some other body. He dressed in wide-lapel suits with tight pegged pants, in the gaudy colors favored by jazz bands of the era.

Since hitting the road at seventeen, Uncle Manzie had lived as he chose. He was a superlative musician, an innovative drummer who played with the Don Redman Orchestra through the 1930s and recorded with Jelly Roll Morton and Louis Armstrong. He was also an incurable free spirit and ne'er-do-well, a carouser who drank up his money, a dangerously handsome rake—Manzie *swang*, in life as in art. By the time we moved in with Grandma Johnson, he was on the slide. He'd killed his big opportunity by showing up drunk for a rehearsal with Duke Ellington and falling off the bandstand. Still and all, he remained a suave hero to an eight-year-old: Mr. Saturday Night in the flesh.

Manzie's wife, my Aunt Margie, had TB and lived mostly in a sanatorium. The care of their only child, a daughter two years older than I, fell to Grandma Johnson by default. But whatever his failures as a father, Manzie was a flamboyantly gifted uncle. Coming home off the road, he'd throw a party that featured his latest blond girlfriend, gales of laughter, and the most beguiling music on his phonograph. Or he'd haul me off to a saloon, set me on a stool, buy me a ginger ale, and pull out his sticks for "paradiddling," a bravura display of percussion. I marveled at my uncle's speed and syncopation, the blur of his nimble wrists as he punished the bar. Whenever a jazzman strutted through the door, Manzie would introduce me. One night I met Erroll Garner.

Uncle Manzie told rousing stories about his antics, like the time the husband got home early in Cleveland (or was it Pittsburgh?), and my uncle had to clamber out the bedroom window and run half-naked down the street. He also filled me in about my father's life as a boy. It was Manzie who related the sad story of Rex, the German shepherd lost in a wager.

"I felt so sorry for Jackie," my uncle said, "but I also thought it was funny, because that dog was so fucking mean that everyone was afraid of it. The only person it liked was your father. I have to admit, I was glad when we got rid of it."

My father looked up to his older brother and envied him, too. Black Jack slaved to win favor in the clock-punching world, and here came Manzie breezing into town, cadging a sawbuck my father couldn't afford to lend, blowing it on a bottle and a prostitute. My uncle had something my dad could not cultivate: charisma. All eyes veered to him when he entered a room, including Grandma Johnson's, who made it blunt that Manzie was her favorite. He could do no wrong. To the plodding younger brother, it just didn't seem fair.

My father was not the same person who'd left New York five years earlier. His time in Washington had embittered him; at thirty-one, his future was dimming. He had trouble retrieving his hack license, and bounced from his janitor's job at Rockefeller Center to per diem work at the General Post Office. "A black man has to do a lot of things to make ends meet," he'd observe, "because he can't count on anything lasting." He was out all the time, which was just as well, as he invariably came home in a foul mood.

I had my own adjustment problems. After reigning at the head of my class at Garfield, I was rudely awakened at P.S. 46, a real school with full-day sessions and certified teachers. In third grade I drew Miss McMahon, a stern young woman who had it in for me. No matter how low I shrank in my seat, she'd call my name and shoot my pulse rate off the charts.

Seeing that I'd fallen behind, my mother stepped up her tutoring. I memorized state capitals till my head spun; I spelled my little heart out. There was steel in

Irene Johnson. When I was cast in a play, she drilled my lines like Otto Preminger.

If I faltered, I bought a one-way ticket to that no-no land, population two: me and my mother's zeal. Once she got so frustrated that she yanked me off the sofa and pinned me to the floor with her knees: *Why can't you learn this?* Even my father considered that a little much. "Come on, Irene," he said, chuckling. "Leave the boy alone."

I was a wreck. By winter I was wetting my bed again.

I judged Miss McMahon unkind for singling me out. But looking back, she might have seen a spark in her timid student, or perhaps a sign of something wrong. A few days before open school night, she called my parents to schedule a conference. As we squeezed into our pint-sized chairs across from the teacher's big desk, she repeated what she'd noted on my report card: "John can't seem to sit still in class. Why do you think he's so nervous?"

My father spread his hands and professed befuddlement. My mother looked away. You could hear the wall clock ticking.

I wanted ever so much to reach out to Miss McMahon at that moment. I burned to blurt out the secret of my father's harsh spankings, of the days when I wiggled on my wooden seat because it hurt too much to sit. (I never thought to indict my mother's Parris Island teaching methods. She was my angel, my infallible one.)

But I didn't trust my teacher, and we had to save face. I was proud of my parents, my family; we were so nice and clean. How could I reveal that I feared my father, that fine-looking man sitting there so affably? Or that I worried about my mother, and what he might do to her?

How could I say that this nice, clean man was a monster? Who would possibly believe it?

I had to keep everything hidden—to dodge trouble,

and to cloak our collective shame. For my father was bound up in us, as were we in him.

I couldn't let on. I couldn't tell on my father. I kept my nervous mouth shut, and no one was the wiser.

The Fifth Avenue double-decker bus let us off at an Everest of steps. Above them, four city blocks long, loomed the Metropolitan Museum of Art. I had no idea what to expect, but I happily held my mother's hand as we ascended into the fortress.

Noting my passion for drawing, my mother had sprung me from school for a private field trip. As we entered the museum's vast lobby, she steered me to the right; she knew her way around. (Had she read about this place? Was she tracing the steps of an old high school outing, or one of my prenatal visits?) When I asked where we were headed, she said, "We're going to ancient Egypt, which was in Africa."

Awestruck, I ran my fingers along the creamy limestone facade of the Tomb of Perneb, a palace bureaucrat from the Fifth Dynasty. My mother said, "This is where brown people were buried in Egypt more than four thousand years ago, and they built great things."

I couldn't fathom how something so old could be more than a mound of dust. "Is it real?" I asked.

"Yes, it's real."

"If it's from Africa, how did it get here?"

"They brought it here," my mother said, skipping the fine points of Western plunder. She led me to an opening at the center of the facade, a passageway so narrow that we had to walk single-file. "Now we're going into this tomb; there are dead people in here."

It scared me to follow her, because the space was so tight that I felt buried, too. We wound up in a tiny, spotlit room with carved wall paintings in vivid greens and ochers—the chapel, my mother explained, where the priests could leave snacks for the resident spirit. The largest painting depicted Perneb, sitting haughtily stiff-backed before an offering table. He was a handsome man with his bronze skin and almond eyes.

My mother had never stopped talking, pointing out this or that. Now her voice dropped to a reverent whisper, as in church. "See how he is?" she said. "Look at his hands. They're just like your father's."

She was right. I knew I'd seen those long, tapered fingers before.

Emboldened, my mother went on, "You ever hear of King Tut? Mama Tutt's name came from the great King Tut."

I said, "What does that mean?"

"It means we're descended from Egyptian royalty, just like this man here. King Tut, Irene Tutt." My mother stood a little taller.

Oh my God, I thought, innocent to the fact that she was making this up as she went along. I felt important, ennobled. For a while I'd want to change my last name from Johnson to Tutt, though I never dared ask my father.

We walked up a grand marble staircase. Then through a broad hallway, decked with so much form and color that I got dizzy as I passed. My mother's commentary was basic: "This is by Rembrandt. He was Dutch, and he was really famous." But to me it was all new and thrilling. The museum was nearly empty, and I remember how clean and orderly it seemed. I remember how special it felt to be amid monumental art and my mother's love all at once. I was whole that day, utterly fed.

She brought me to a room of huge classical paintings. There, filling one entire wall, hung a picture so real that I thought I was inside it.

I forgot all about cousin Perneb's tomb; *The Horse Fair* crippled me in my tracks. The canvas seemed as wide as a movie screen. Along a tree-lined Parisian boulevard, a dozen muscular Percherons were led through their paces in a ring. Here was an anatomy of horses— trotting, galloping, rearing from every angle. They were mighty, thick-legged creatures, made for the plow or to port knights to battle. At the center bucked a mighty white stallion, raging and red-eyed, its forelegs pawing three feet off the ground.

Though the sky above them hung slate and overcast, the Percherons' coats were burnished, as if lit from within. The entire composition was magical to me, in the sense that magic is something impossible. I couldn't comprehend how anyone could paint such a thing, though I knew well how someone could love horses so much.

"How did he do this?" I said.

"No, a woman did it. Rosa Bonheur." My mother sounded pleased for her gender.

I could have stared at *The Horse Fair* for hours, and it took some vigorous coaxing to get me to leave for home. For an anxious child, the Metropolitan was a place to breathe. I would dream about getting locked inside at night, and it was a good dream. I could hide and live there, and be safe.

The Tutts weren't especially religious, and neither was my father. Grandma Johnson, though, was a dyed-in-the-wool Baptist, like a lot of folks from the South, and she made it her pious duty to drag my mother and me to St. James. While the gospel music was fine, we never got used to the style of worship. When the members fell out for the Holy Ghost, I'd be startled by their bursts of rapture. Why did they have to be so loud? My mother and I would look at each other, strangers in a strange land.

After the service, the ladies stood outside in their Sunday finest, stylin' in their fancy hats. My mother never put them down, exactly, but she knew that she didn't fit in. She lacked the wardrobe or interest to compete.

Fair-skinned women vexed Grandma Johnson to begin with; she regarded them as snobs. My mother sealed the deal by converting to the Catholic Church. After we'd taken our Sunday business elsewhere, I'd hear my grandmother grumbling, "Why do you have to be different?"

My mother paid no mind. She liked the hushed rituals of Catholicism, the privacy of confession, the freedom from fashion codes. The Church would be one more thing we shared apart from everyone else.

I was duly baptized and enrolled for instruction at the Church of St. Catherine of Genoa on 153rd Street, a modest brick structure in scale with the adjacent brownstones. No soaring spires or voice-of-God organ—just two dozen rows of benches, a few stained glass windows, and a tarnished brass altar rail.

Even so, I could barely stand when called to the rail for my First Holy Communion. As with everything else, I fretted about doing it precisely right. You had to let the Host dissolve on your tongue, no chewing allowed. Above all, you did not want to regurgitate. An altar boy held a small pallet under your mouth, so if you spit up the body of Christ, you'd have a second chance. I saw more than one kid gag that morning, but the pallet blessedly stayed out of play.

They had some rugged nuns at Our Lady of the Rosary. It didn't take much to cross them—a yawn, a wrong answer—and their punishment was swift and sure, a vicious rap across the knuckles with a wooden pointer. They had the other kids petrified, but they didn't scare me. I never cried in Catholic school; I'd survived much worse at home. Besides, I was eager to learn, and to believe.

One day I asked our teacher, "What's heaven like?"

"It's like a vacation you never want to come back from."

And I said, "What's a vacation?" My family had never taken one.

The nun explained that heaven was glorious all the time, a place where good conquered evil at last. For a put-upon boy, that was the Church's greatest gift: the faith that justice would visit us, if only down the road. Because I knew that my mother and I were good, and I knew something about evil, too.

It was gaining on us all the time.

Displaced and disheartened, my mother took to drinking more often. My father's jealousy, meanwhile, spun out of control. We were at Mama Tutt's one evening when the local numbers runner came by, a dapper fellow named Emmett. After he left, my father bawled out his wife for coming on to the man, an insane accusation. My mother was the friendliest, most outgoing person in the world. She liked to play the numbers and could be a sloppy drunk. But she was incapable of flirting; she lacked the coyness for it, the calculation. She was true blue, and deep down my father knew it.

The truth didn't stop him, though. My mother was the one thing of value in his life, and he assumed in his self-hatred that the world sought to steal her away. A glance from another man could set him off, but that was just the ground floor. He begrudged my mother's closeness with her family. He resented her friends.

At bottom, he was jealous of her joy.

On the subway home that night, heedless of strangers' stares, he dressed her down: "Why did you talk to him that way, Irene? You and your sister, you drink and get loose and start flirting with every man in sight." (My father drank, too, but never lost control. He only got meaner.)

Back home he stormed up the stairs, still railing at my mother's indiscretions. I gripped her hand as she followed. My father got louder, and I began to cry. As we reached the top of the stairway, on the landing between Grandma Johnson and Uncle Manzie, tension crackled in the air like heat lightning.

My father erupted—"You were fresh with that man!"—and loosed a roundhouse slap to my mother's face. Her head snapped back and ricocheted off the wall.

I was horrified. I'd seen him slap her before, but not like that, not with such lunatic distemper. My mother was too pretty to hurt, even if she drank too much. I wailed, "Don't hit my mama! Please don't hit my mama!"

"Shut up!" my father said, and my head exploded as I took his next shot.

Still unsteady on her feet, groaning in pain, my mother said, "No, Jackie, don't hit him."

"Shut up, goddamn it, shut *up*," and he slapped her again.

I shrank back toward Grandma Johnson's door as my mother sidled forward to shield me. We were trapped between a locked apartment and a crazy man, and I was eight years old and there was nothing I could do.

My father yelled, "You were fresh with Emmett!" and charged. My mother cried out; I was shrieking bloody murder. The door behind me flew open and someone seized me from behind. I turned my head—

It was Spiderman!

Aaagh! I screamed.

"What's going on out there?" Roused from her bed by the ruckus, Grandma Johnson stood glaring from the doorway in her nightgown. A black hairnet stretched down to her eyebrows. I'd never seen the creepy thing before, and I'd be a happy little boy if I never had to see it again.

My mother's eye was already swollen. Grandma Johnson looked at her disgustedly and said, "Oh, Irene, you're drunk again." A teetotaler herself, she deemed my mother's drinking unseemly.

"Yeah, she's drunk again," my father said, as if that explained everything.

Holding me close, Grandma Johnson said, "You better stop this right now. If you two are going to get drunk and fight, you'll have to move out of here."

My grandmother ushered me into the kitchen. To get the last word, my father shoved my mother in after us. She tumbled through the door and sprawled to her knees. When she tried to get up, her ankle gave and she fell again, this time backward, in a flailing trajectory beyond my father's grasp. She looked almost funny, like the scarecrow taking a pratfall on the yellow brick road, except this was *my mother,* and her poor head was flying straight toward Grandma Johnson's metal-topped table.

It was like watching a car crash—or, more, like having one. She fell in slow motion, missing the table by inches on her way to the floor. Her audience stood breathless, helpless. Wrapped in my grandma's arms, I knew it would be bad. My mother was about to split her head. My mother was about to die.

She struck the linoleum so hard that her head bounced and hit a second time. My father knelt at her side, his rage a vapor: *Oh Irene, oh baby baby I'm so sorry baby . . .*

Remarkably, she was dazed but still conscious. Aside from her eye, she seemed unhurt. She looked up at her husband with her sweetest smile and said, "That's all right, honey, that's all right."

In a strange, throaty voice, my father said something I'd never heard from him before: "I love you, baby." He sat down next to her on the kitchen floor, sobbing convulsively, squeezing her tight.

My mother said, "I love you, too."

At that point the scene goes white for me, but I remember how confused I was to see my mother comforting *him*. But then she knew how much he needed her. She knew because she felt the same way.

They were all they had. They were in love.

By morning the bruise covered half my mother's face, with a hand mark branded on her cheek. I couldn't even offer my sympathy; her plight was too awful to be acknowledged. Speaking not a word, she shuffled through the flat in her fraying bathrobe to serve her man's breakfast. My irrepressible mother had been pacified. Diminished. Curbed like a dog who'd been kicked once too often.

That was the sickest part of our drama: the morning after. When the adrenaline and alcohol metabolized, and the dust settled like fallout, and we had to go on together, the three of us. That was the part I came to dread the most.

As my father chewed his Wonder Bread toast, still smoldering over Emmett, I regarded him knowingly. The stain of my dislike for him darkened. It was turning into something close to hatred.

After the incident on the stairwell, it was as though my father's emotional governor—long prone to failure—had burned out for good. He began battering my mother on a regular basis, maybe once or twice a week. It usually happened at dinner, before Grandma Johnson got home from her service downtown. He might start with a slow burn or a quick fit; his flash point ignited at random. We walked on eggshells all the time.

I knew when the *bang* was coming. Though I'd delay the inevitable by asking for the milk or mashed potatoes, I could not derail him. If I got too pesky, he'd warn me to shut up. Defeated, I'd seek my mother's eyes to show how sorry I was, and how much I loved her.

And I told myself, *When I get bigger, I'll get him back.*

Then—and it always shocked me, no matter how many times I'd seen it—came the deluge. My father's massive hand whipped through the air and met my mother flush in the face. "Oh my God!" she'd cry. "Oh Jackie, no!" There might be a single blow or a hail of them, depending on what it took to knock the woman from her chair. To make his point.

I can scarcely convey what it was like to see my mother smashed senseless to the floor, her wavy hair spilling from its bun, her housedress flown open. When I summon the image, fifty years later, I feel much as I did then: fearful, furious, impotent, disgraced.

When it was over, my mother would excuse herself to the bathroom, where she'd stay with the cold water running. It could be a long time before she came out, longer still before she'd be herself again.

My father never broke my mother's arm or so much as a finger. His assaults were meant to degrade and control, and my mother did her part to keep them private. When she suffered a black eye or an especially lurid contusion, she trotted out the old clichés. She'd fallen. She'd struck her face on a doorknob. The stories made no sense, and her listeners knew the truth anyway.

What kind of a man would take a woman he loved, take her energy and zest and her power and juice, and crush it down to nothing?

It's a daunting question, all in all. If you are the man's son, you might need most of a lifetime to find your answer.

While television was new and beyond our budget, we did own a small radio, a plastic brown box with a narrow bandwidth. But *The Lone Ranger* came in loud and clear each Wednesday at 7:30, and what else did a boy need? I looked forward to the program all week; it was my gangplank, my portal. From the first trumpet peals of the *William Tell* overture, with those galloping hooves in the background, I was in a trance. You could have stuck me with a knitting needle and I wouldn't have noticed.

One Wednesday my father came home in a funk and got into it with my mother. The fight had nothing to do with me, but his malice sifted through the flat like a gas leak. I had a premonition that he might impose the ultimate punishment: no *Lone Ranger*. (He'd threatened this once before, when he quizzed me on my spelling and I messed up on "Mississippi.") I remember begging to Jesus that he wouldn't go that far.

Sadly, Jesus turned a deaf ear that evening. "And you can just *forget* about your show tonight," my father said, frowning at the radio. "I've been busting my hump all day, and I'm not going to have that damn noise in the house."

I could not believe it. As show time neared and my father would not soften, I wandered into the kitchen, disconsolate. Down the next street, across a back alley, someone had a window open. Above the city's static rose the unmistakable clarion: *Da-da-dum, da-da-dum . . .*

I cocked my ear toward the distant radio. Squinting my eyes shut, I could make out my hero's *Hi-Yo Silver, away!* I heard the five staggered gunshots—the Lone Ranger always fired second, and last—before the announcer broke in: *A fiery horse with a speed of light, a cloud of dust, and a hearty "Hi-Yo, Silver!" The Lone Ranger!*

This might not be so bad, I thought.

With his faithful Indian companion, Tonto, the masked rider of the plains led the fight for law and order in the agrarian western United States . . . The episode began with tense news from Dan, the Lone

Ranger's nephew. A ruthless cattle baron was cooking a bullet breakfast for a bunch of poor settlers. I heard another *Hi-Yo, Silver!* and the Lone Ranger was off, with Tonto on his heels. (*Git 'em up, Scout!*)

But I never found out what happened to the settlers, or how the Lone Ranger eluded certain death, because my neighbors turned down their radio. Strain as I might, I heard naught but muffled laughter and traffic sounds, and the plaint of a stray cat.

My father made a mistake that night. In the fullness of time I would block out most of his beatings and much of his terror against my mom. But I wouldn't forget the night I lost *The Lone Ranger.* No, I could not forgive him for that.

Mama Tutt and Aunt Marian were fed up with their bellicose in-law. "He's no good, Fatty," they said. "You got to get out."

A year after our return from Washington, my mother relented. She found a job at Woolworth's and moved us in with her family on 148th Street, a dozen blocks away.

The living was better, a two-bedroom apartment on the sixth floor of an elevator building. My mother shared Mama Tutt's bed, with my fold-up cot set alongside. Aunt Marian had the other bedroom with her husband, Sylvester Mosely, and my cousin Dianne, two years younger than I.

I was ecstatic when my parents split up; I awoke each day with a sense of relief. I loved my relatives dearly, especially Mama Tutt. A stocky woman about as tall as my mother, she hot-combed her hair in a tight curl in the front, after Billie Holiday. She loved her hooch and a game of bid whist, at which she cheated freely, but most of all she loved her twin daughters. She distrusted husbands on principle. No man was good enough for her girls—certainly not my father, not even my Uncle Syl, whom Mama Tutt goaded and hounded and, some years later, finally drove away.

Which seemed to me a pity, because Sylvester Mosely was wonderful. A Pullman porter on the Pennsylvania Railroad, a leftist union board member, he was a compact man who moved with fluid grace. (He'd starred in the sixty-yard dash at DeWitt Clinton High School, and was fast enough to win a tryout with the U.S. Olympic team.) Always ready for his next train, he'd be neat as a pin in a crisp shirt and tie, his nails impeccably trimmed, his spectacles rubbed till they sparkled.

Uncle Syl was a voluminous reader, a self-educated man who later worked his way through City College and ultimately enrolled at Oxford University. When the living room grew too rowdy, he'd retreat to his bedroom haven and his collection of classical music. One day he crooked a finger at me to follow him. He pulled a shiny black disc from its sleeve and placed it on his record player. He said, "I want you to listen to something."

It was the New York Philharmonic playing *La Valse,* Ravel's study in grand abandon, and it ran away with me. My parents stayed current with the likes of Sarah Vaughan and Billy Eckstine, and I knew instrumental jazz through Uncle Manzie. But I had no idea that music could have such heft and sweep or come at you in Technicolor. At the end, when the piece swirled to frenzy and nearly burst, I was speechless.

Smiling down at me, Uncle Syl said *La Valse* reminded him of a recent movie, *The Specter of the Rose,* "where these two ballet dancers are partners, and they fall in love. But the man goes crazy and leaps out of a hotel window"—my uncle tossed off a homespun *grand jeté*— "and he holds his position all the way down." What tragedy! What romance! It would be twenty years or more before I actually got to see the film, but the ending played just as I'd pictured it.

When Uncle Syl saw how *La Valse* had affected me, he gave me the record. It instantly became my proudest possession.

My uncle was, I suppose, all my father was not: mild-mannered, considerate, ambitious. Naturally, Black Jack couldn't stand him. With little to criticize, he'd assail Uncle Syl's frugality: "Aw, he's just a cheap nigger."

In my hurt I tried to show him that I loved Syl better. When my father came around, I'd laugh extra loud at my uncle's puns, act especially keen to play our word games. Did my father notice? Was he wounded? I cannot be sure, but it wasn't for my lack of trying.

Three months after we left him, my father took off for Denver and a fresh start. I hardly noticed. Life was looking up, especially after my relatives opened a candy store on St. Nicholas Avenue, across the street from P.S. 46. Aunt Marian worked the soda fountain, while Mama Tutt staffed the candy counter. Given my grandmother's sweet tooth, it was asking the fox to audit the henhouse. When Uncle Syl returned from the rails, he'd inventory his stock, shake his head at Mama Tutt, and say with a sigh, "You're eating up all the profits."

The candy store was my Xanadu, a trove of wonderment and delight. It was there that I got addicted to chocolate malteds, slipped to me each day after school. And it was there that I came to know Emmett, numbers man extraordinaire.

In a way, Emmett and my father were alter egos, physically interchangeable pieces. They were both tall and slender, ramrod straight, with similar coloring. On the rare occasions when my father dressed up, he'd actually look like Emmett, because Emmett was always dressed up. He wasn't flashy, just natty and *au courant,* from his dark gray fedora (the brim bent down just so) to his fine navy wool overcoat, hemmed fashionably near his shoe tops.

Three times a day, Emmett plied his trade by the candy store. He arrived without fail, in all weather, though I can't recall the rain ever falling on Emmett. He stood cool and expressionless, scouting up and down the block for his clientele. Every so often a person came by and passed something into his palm, the transaction so smooth that you'd miss it if you blinked.

When the New York Giants played a home game at the nearby Polo Grounds, I'd join Emmett outside for some commerce of my own. Darting along the street, I'd steer people to free parking spots and hope for a dime tip. As a man who esteemed a good hustle, Emmett threw me his spare change.

Before moving to his next station, the runner dropped by the store to see Mama Tutt. A serious numbers player, my grandmother wouldn't part with a quarter before consulting her book on numerology and the "Ching Chow" column in the tabloids. I knew that Emmett wasn't there for the cherry phosphates, and posted myself at the door as a lookout. If any cops headed our way, I'd duck in my head and shout, "Here come the bulls!" Mama Tutt would clear her research off the counter while Emmett pocketed the betting slips.

Not long after my father left for Colorado, his worst nightmare came to pass. Emmett invited my mother out and she accepted. When he came to pick her up, I noticed how nicely he treated her. I don't know if their liaison went further than a night on the town, but I wouldn't have minded if it had. Emmett might have been a marginal figure, but I never heard a harsh word from him, never saw the back of his hand.

CHAPTER THREE

MY FATHER WAS NO GOOD BY HIMSELF. AFTER SIX WEEKS IN DEN-ver he folded. He returned to New York and his room at Grandma Johnson's, and begged my mother to come back to him.

He found her of a mood to listen. While our days had been infinitely less fraught, and my mother wasn't drink-ing so much, she seemed duller than I was used to. She went slack. As painful as it could be to live with her hus-band, she'd learned that she could not live without him.

As we were two extra mouths to feed, our relatives felt free to preach from the Gospel of Saint I-Told-You-So. Mama Tutt would tell my mother, "You're better off with-out that son of a bitch."

And: "You never should have married him anyway."

And: "That Jackie was a no-good black bastard from the start, uh-*huh*."

Poor Fatty took it in the neck, and it killed her. It's fair to say that my grandmother was stronger-willed, Aunt Mar-ian more disciplined and realistic. But my mother could be obstinate when pressured. The family's diatribe would push her back to my father that much sooner, if only to prove her critics wrong. She would stand by her man.

One night we went to Grandma Johnson's and stayed over. After my parents thought I was asleep, I heard them getting lovey-dovey. They quieted for a time, and then my mother said, "I can't come back here and live with your mother, and I know you can't stay with *my* mother."

And my father said, "Well, we don't have enough money for our own place, but we've got to figure out something." The next morning he set about apartment hunting in Brooklyn, where rents were cheaper.

As I track the course of my parents' lives, I wonder at my mother's decision to reunite with a man she knew to be harmful, if not downright dangerous. Given her looks and smarts, she might have done so much better, even with a young son.

But my mother had been broken and saw no place for repair. It was as though her identity had frozen when she met Jackie Johnson on Edgecombe Avenue. Her stunted ego subsumed to his. When my father put her in that two-dollar wedding dress, he hadn't just married her. He'd *rescued* her. They were tied in ways no one else could fathom.

As Mama Tutt would say to me, "If your father coughs, your mother gets pneumonia."

In this bleak time for my parents, any change seemed positive. Children tending to be optimists, I got caught up in our move in spite of myself. We were like a pride of lions, a unit of three against the world.

Still, it was a sad day for me when my mother and father reconciled. Because it is only a matter of time before papa lion turns on the cub to destroy him, to bring the female back into heat.

To have her all to himself.

My father must have sniffed my ambivalence, because he did something out of character. He took me out on the town, just the two of us, just for fun.

Our excursion was a day trip to heaven. At Radio City Music Hall, the most majestic space I'd ever seen, we came in time for the matinee. I can remember the gigantic screen, the surging soundtrack, but I cannot tell you the film we saw that day. What I've kept is what came after.

As the grand curtain closed, the Radio City orchestra tiptoed into Ravel's *Bolero.* A sequined woman pranced across the colossal stage with a drummer tight behind her. They were followed by more drummers and more meltingly limber dancers—the Rockettes! The music got louder and louder. The stage was filled with manic banging and leggy synchronicity. Troupes of drummers packed the loge boxes overhead; the pounding came at us from all angles. As the piece swelled to its climax, the Rockettes kicking to the moon, I felt sensually glutted, as close to carnal satisfaction as a nine-year-old can get.

(*Bolero* may be a bit of a joke now, adored by dilettantes the world over. As Ravel himself wrote before he died, "Too bad there is no music in it." But you cannot say a bad word about *Bolero* to me.)

After the show we hiked through Rockefeller Center, pausing on a walkway that overlooked the sunken skating rink. I can still see my father beside me, so long and slim with his dark chocolate skin, such a good-looking man. It must have been late January or February, because the giant Christmas tree had been trucked away. But other attractions lay in store.

My father said, "Do you know what that is?" He pointed to a gleaming object that rose out of a fountain beyond the rink. In a plaza filled with marvels, this was the boldest one of all: a man of gold flying through the air, his robes billowing behind him, a flaming torch in hand.

I said, "That's a statue," and stared at it some more. The flier had a lean swimmer's build. You could count his ribs. You could see the tendons in his arms and ankles; you could see each lock of his upswept hair, miming the strands of fire in his fist.

After pausing for effect, my father poked out his chest and said, "That's Prometheus. I cleaned that thing."

And I thought, *Wow, my dad cleaned Prometheus!* I was bowled over. When my father worked here, I'd pictured him as a custodian who scoured the bathrooms, like the one who wheeled the bucket at my school. But my dad had done nothing of the sort. He'd been part of something miraculous. For me, it was as though he had helped *make* the statue. I thought it was the finest thing a man could do.

We crossed to the other side of the rink to the RCA Building, a great wall of steel and granite, so tall that I couldn't sight the top of it. My father said mysteriously, "Do you want to see the fourth dimension?" I had no idea what he was talking about, but I was game. He led me into the lobby and said, "Look up." I took a gander at a bare-chested man staring back at me from the center of the high ceiling. Drawn with huge muscles, he was hauling a tree bough that might have daunted Paul Bunyan.

My father said, "Now walk this way, and watch him move."

As I paced toward the far wall, a curious thing happened. The man in the mural seemed to shift his weight and follow me with his eyes! It was my first brush with trompe l'oeil, and I actually gasped. I traversed every art deco floor tile in that lobby, my neck craning till it ached, and the man watched my every step.

"What is he doing?" I asked, after my feet began hurting.

My dad looked at me and said, "This is all about the workers, the people who worked hard. You know, Johnny, the people who built everything in this country were poor working people." Though not a great reader, my father leafed through the left-leaning daily *P.M.* and greatly admired Paul Robeson. I thought he was the smartest man in the world to be able to explain all of this.

That was a singular day for me, a furlough from poverty and into a new realm. It was also the nicest time I'd ever spend with my father. He was soft that whole afternoon. He put aside everything hounding him to be with his son, body and soul. At one point—was it at Radio City or by Prometheus, or under the magic mural?—a funny sensation stole over me. I became aware of how much I had missed my father. I might have missed him when he'd been in Denver, I suppose, but I'd really missed him all my life. In Rockefeller Center I found an intelligent, thoughtful man who observed the world around him and passed his wisdom to his child.

I missed the father he should have been.

We landed on Macon Street, in the heart of Bedford-Stuyvesant. "Your daddy and I are going to make a go of it," my mother assured me. "Everything will be fine."

When I first saw our new block, it seemed nice enough. Our building was a Victorian brownstone with a carved bay window, a grand domicile in its time, before the landlord chopped it into four ill-kept rentals plus a communal kitchen. I got suspicious in the creepy foyer, with its musty smell and soiled green carpeting. When I saw our one-room apartment—the front parlor on the second floor, with a bath outside in the dim hallway—my heart sank. Everything was *worse.* Even at Grandma Johnson's, we didn't share a kitchen with strangers. I didn't have to pee in a milk bottle at night for fear of bumping into someone scary.

As soon as I saw the place, I knew I didn't want to be there.

My parents set about installing our few possessions.

Their double bed went in one front corner, my cot in the other. We had a single chest of drawers, a few mismatched wooden chairs, and a threadbare sofa with a broken spring, a hand-me-down from Mama Tutt.

Our floors were blue and orange linoleum, except where they'd worn through to the black backing. (In my experience, there was no such thing as new linoleum.) A window seat bridged the beds, but I can't remember any sunshine there. It was always gray on Macon Street.

If my new home was dismal, my new school was alarming. No one had a tougher reputation than the kids from Bed-Stuy; in Harlem they'd inspired many an urban legend. When I walked into P.S. 70, I had the gait of a condemned man.

As a midyear transfer, I was left to the mercies of a sixth-grade "monitor." His job was to escort me to my classroom. Halfway there, he strong-armed my twelve cents in lunch money and left me in the corridor, shaken and lost.

In a caste system of ability tracks, I was thrown into a fourth grade of middling achievers. My bright spot was my guidance counselor, a young black woman as fair-skinned as my mother, but with a middle-class polish. Mrs. Purvis was the first teacher to encourage me. She corrected my speech, pushed me to read and to think. She'd say, "You can do better than that." I responded like a parched plant to a water pot.

My father, meanwhile, was back to hacking in a Checker cab, in addition to his temp work at the post office. He'd excitedly describe his celebrity fares: Humphrey Bogart, Cary Grant, Spencer Tracy and Katharine Hepburn. (Bogie was the best tipper, because he'd always had a few.) But my dad would be less talkative other nights, when he finished a shift with three or four dollars in his pocket.

He worked all the time, and none of his jobs required

so much skill as skating backward. As the strain told on him, he took it out on my mother. He knew of her fling with Emmett and couldn't let it rest. There were lots of bad feelings cooped up in our apartment, and no Grandma Johnson to moderate.

Soon enough, old patterns were renewed: the slaps, the screams. Those leaden mornings after, like winter in the summertime. My father hit me, too, but I was small game. He saved his best licks for my mother, which was more excruciating for me than being beaten myself. I so wanted to protect her; I felt guilty when I couldn't even try. I became a careful, watchful, worried child, a pint-sized sentinel in over his head.

Were it not for the photographic evidence—a snowman under construction, a pail and shovel at the seashore—I could not swear to you that I ever was a child.

Most evenings, my mother and I would snuggle in her bed. We'd take turns reading aloud from *Tom Sawyer* or *Huckleberry Finn,* the same books over and over, laughing together at the same parts every time. I envied Tom and Huck their mischief and liberty, and most of all their father-free existence. I identified more with Tom, because I had my mother to care for me, as Tom had Aunt Polly. I had no thought to run away.

I wished that my father would run instead, as he had to Colorado. And this time never come back.

When I rationalize what happened to my family, I look at it this way. My father was a black man come of age in the Depression, lacking special talents and habitually aggrieved. If he didn't feed off his resentments, he would starve. He couldn't abuse his boss at the post office. He wouldn't wallop the guy at the next bar stool; that wasn't his style, and the outcome was too dicey. Where could he go with his anger? Who could he assault? It was simple, really. He'd go home and beat my mother and me.

When I stop trying to rationalize, I look at it this way: My father was as evil as a snake.

It was worse for my mother on the weekends, when he'd been drinking. It was worse for me when he came home from work pissed off and stone sober. In Brooklyn my beatings took on a ritual quality, like Kabuki or animal sacrifice. I knew the choreography cold.

I remember one time on Macon Street, shortly after we moved there. It has stayed with me, I guess, because my bitterness bloomed so vividly then. My parents had promised that everything would be fine once they got back together, and nothing was fine. We lived in a hovel, with less money than ever. I'd swapped my nice Harlem school and chocolate malteds for *Blackboard Jungle* and the backwater of Bedford-Stuyvesant. I was one disillusioned child.

We could gauge my father's mood the instant he came through the door. When he entered with a smile, everything was great. I'd be ultra-happy. I'd laugh too loud, run a little wild. *We're okay, we're okay, Daddy's in a good mood today!* I might ask about last night's prizefight, and he'd show me a boxing move. And I would love my mother and my father, the best parents in the whole wide world.

But when my father hulked in curt and dismissive, barely speaking, we knew what that meant, too. It was his preamble to violence.

On one such afternoon, I was doing my lessons on the window seat, with my mother up and down the stairs to cook dinner while checking my progress. I could see what lay in store by the curl of my father's mouth. He was spoiling for a fight. My mother and I turned quiet and submissive, like wolves showing their necks to the alpha male. But we knew it was going to happen no matter what we did. One of us was going to get it.

My mother took the middle seat at the table that day, with her men at either end. Was she trying, instinctively, to buffer me? If so, she would pay.

Once he'd appeased his stomach, my father ended the suspense. I don't recall what I did or said, but he leaned across the table and struck me in the face, ramming into my mother on course. She recoiled and cried, "Jackie, *no!*," loud enough for all in the house to hear.

I was knocked backward, clear out of my seat. But I didn't stay down long; I didn't dare miss my cue. I scrambled to my feet and raced down the slick wooden stairway, hoping not to land on my head.

By that point my father was a one-man police riot. He lurched one stride behind me, tugging at his leather belt while slapping at me from behind. I shrieked and tore at my clothes: *No, Daddy, no!* I headed straight for our room: Do not pass Go. I wasn't fleeing my father. I was running to take my medicine.

I was running to my doom.

Bringing up the rear, my mother cajoled him softly, "Please, Jackie, don't." She knew she had to lay back. If she said too much, it could make things worse for me. If she'd grabbed my father's arm, he would have beaten her inside out.

I ran into the far corner and flung myself on my parents' bed. I fumbled with the last of my clothing, dying to get it over with. But my father couldn't wait. He whipped my arms even as I unzipped my pants and bent to my socks, slowing me considerably.

At last he had what he craved: my complete subjugation. I lay naked full-length on my stomach, sick with déjà vu, facing out toward the man who'd laughed with me—was it only that morning?—over oatmeal. I forced my eyes open because I needed to see what he was doing. I had to keep a watch on this crazy man in case he went too far and I had to get away.

I saw my father's hand, his beautiful hand. I saw the flat black belt, doubled for precision, paused at its apogee. I saw a flash of my mother in the background; she'd be careful not to crowd him.

Then the hand came down, and the belt whizzed through the air, and my bottom caught fire.

My father went to work in a fever. He beat me up and down, homing in from the midpoint of my buttocks to just above the backs of my knees. Where the flesh was softest, where the evidence would be safe from prying eyes.

Please Daddy don't oh no please please . . .

My hearing clicked on and off, from din to dead quiet and back. Even so, I know that I screamed out at each lash. I know that I begged him to stop. I can still feel my body writhing to find refuge. The movement was involuntary, from my spinal cord more than my brain.

And I remember my father commanding, "Don't move! You lie still and take it like a man!"

Bawling uncontrollably, I would try my best to lie still. I was stuck in a catch-22. The more I resisted, even passively, the longer and harder he would beat me. But it's a tall order for a fourth-grader to take it like a man when a grown-up is dancing all over you.

Gradually, with supreme effort, I tamed myself. My crying quelled to a heaving whimper. My father fed on the first jolt of energy, the momentum of the chase, the wrangling of his prey. Once I was subdued, the sport went out of it. The light came back inside his head. His whip hand slowed, finally stopped.

His demons were fed. He'd found his release.

I hated the aftershock worst of all. For several minutes, with my diaphragm in spasm, I fought for a steady breath. Then I sat up, red-eyed and pathetic. There we were, the three of us, all messed up and nowhere to go. We moved in a vacuum, a bad dream state, a nothingness so thick it could be sliced.

I hobbled out to the bathroom to pull my underpants back on. When I returned and slid onto my cot, my mother came over—*slow approach, slow approach, don't set him off again*—with a white washcloth and alcohol to soothe my welts. There would be no *Tom Sawyer* that night.

I went to sleep aquiver, wishing my father were dead.

Against all odds, the next day came. I began that torturous climb up the evolutionary trail to where I could be human again and not an animal. I tried to find my way back to decency as quickly as I could. I needed—we all needed—to rebuild some semblance of family.

But how do you go on with one another? How do you segue from a felony to a game of Chinese checkers? *Okay, let's dry those tears and have some fun now.* Just how is that a rational thing to do?

To show he wasn't feeling guilty, my father ignored me the next morning. Rather than apologize, he lectured me after school: "As the head of this house, I've got to do the right thing here. If you spare the rod, you can spoil the child."

I knew his game and found it infuriating. I tuned him out and moved as far away as our parlor would allow. Only now do I see why he bothered to justify what he'd done. He wanted me to love him, in spite of everything.

He just wanted me to love him.

If I drew a moral from my whippings, it wasn't the one on Dad's lesson plan. I deduced that my father was one mean dude. I loved him and I hated him, but above all I'd beware of him. I had to be careful, because he would hurt me.

It is one thing to discover that your father's not a god.

It is another to know that he is villainous. Somewhere deep inside me, a rickety little person kept striving to be a good boy, the best boy, at any cost.

But it was also a steely little person. When I willed myself to calmness in the eye of my father's storm, I gained something invaluable. I learned that you can reason yourself to a higher path, even when the options seem grim. There is always a choice that's a tiny bit better, and sometimes that tiny bit can save your life.

CHAPTER FOUR

FOR MY TENTH BIRTHDAY, IN JUNE OF 1948, MY FATHER TOOK ME to Ebbets Field: my first ball game, a landmark event. I idolized Jackie Robinson, a sensation in his second year in the big leagues. Plus I loved getting out with my dad, which didn't happen too often.

The stadium thrummed with the chatter of tens of thousands. Under a solstice sun, the colors were astounding, hallucinogenic. I had never seen grass that green or uniforms that white. We had seats by the Dodger dugout on the first base side, so close that you could spot the tobacco bulge in the players' cheeks. When the home team took the field and the crowd stood cheering as one, I was swept away in shared emotion.

As the infielders warmed up, I marveled at Robinson's poise. On that storied diamond, he took grounders like everyone else, as though there were nothing to it. Then the Dodgers came to bat, my hero leading off. I leaned forward, enthralled—

"Hey, Robinson, ya bum!" jeered a white fan just behind us. When his buddies joined the heckling, I was shocked. Didn't everyone root for the Dodgers in Brooklyn? Didn't everyone love Jackie Robinson? As my father began to take exception, a rollicking cheer drowned him out. Robinson had singled! Jackie sprinted down the line before us, pigeon-toed and powerful, breathtakingly swift. After rounding the bag with thrilling insolence to dare a throw, he sauntered back to the base like its rightful owner.

The Dodgers wound up winning the game, but that one at-bat was enough for me. The next day I walked pigeon-toed to school and ran pigeon-toed at punchball, and I wondered: Did anyone notice how much faster I'd become?

In the middle of fifth grade we moved to a larger apartment on Gates Avenue, half a dozen blocks north. While still sharing a kitchen and hallway bath, we now had three rooms to ourselves, with a narrow one for me at the front. The extra space was therapeutic; my father wasn't so Vesuvian all the time.

We weren't exactly moving on up, however. Our new block was a file of sagging row houses, one long heap of rotting wood and chipped asbestos siding. On Gates Avenue we touched bottom.

Our street funneled traffic to the Interboro Parkway. When the major arteries clogged, streams of cars were diverted past my house on their way to Long Island. I'd stand at the curb and watch the glossy, late-model Buicks and Pontiacs—real novelties in Bedford-Stuyvesant—crawl by a few feet from my nose. I'd peer at the white couples inside, with their windows rolled up and their anxious eyes and their fingers feeling for the door locks.

I didn't realize that they were looking at me; they were frightened of *me*. They'd pegged me as a vandal, or worse, and they knew there were more where I came from. They missed the little boy who'd never think to do them harm.

It didn't occur to them that I itched to escape, too.

Postwar prosperity somehow skipped Gates Avenue. Our poverty pressed most heavily at night, when my block became a netherworld of cheap highs and not-so-quiet desperation. People flocked the sidewalks in all but the bitterest weather, drinking from clear bottles and hunting for dispute. I witnessed women fighting hand to hand, no holds barred. I saw a woman stabbed by a man and fall bleeding to the ground. I remember a father chasing his own child down the street, a knife bobbing in his fist.

One white family still resided on the block. They were sinister and exotic, the toughest bunch of white folks you would ever want to meet.

We split the second floor with a vague number of shady grown-ups who slept in the back room. As far as we could tell, they lacked a single steady job among them. After roosting on our stoop at all hours, they'd stumble into the hallway with heavy feet and bad language. I steered clear of them as best I could, and kept my milk bottle handy after dark.

Here is what Gates Avenue was like for me: I was afraid of the people outside, and more afraid of the people inside, and most of all I feared my father. Danger lurked at every turn, at any hour.

We lived in the middle of the block, between Patchen and Ralph, the commercial drag where I'd catch the trolley to P.S. 70. I felt slightly safer that way, walking in the shadow of the 20th Precinct station house. On the other hand, it was chancy to call the cops with a problem. They'd arrive with an attitude if they came at all, swaggering out of their squad cars to bully people along: "Get a move on, nigger."

After my father left for the post office we closed and locked our door. My mother would tuck me in bed and sometimes linger, to huddle against the night sounds. I felt safer enfolded in our old fetal embrace. But I found it unnerving that she seemed worried, too.

It was after midnight in the cool of autumn when something jerked me awake. By the time I reached my window to look out, my mother was running to me. When I asked what was happening, she touched a finger to her lips: *Shhh* . . . We knelt at the low sill in my darkened room, hardly breathing.

Bathed in the street's half-light, a dark blue sedan rolled forward in gear, ever so slowly. It wove down the middle of the deserted block, still east of us but coming our way. The rear door of the driver's side swung open. There, hanging on to the window frame, was the source of the animal sound: a slim young woman, naked as day. Only her right leg remained inside the car. She was hopping on the other like an injured bird, her mouth wide and round in a scream that would not stop.

As the sedan came even with our house, I could make out a driver . . . a second man next to him . . . a third in the rear. *Lord!* They were punching the woman from every angle. The one in back reached over to slam the door shut on her poor leg, again and again. With each dull thud she huffed in pain, yet hung on. As hard as the men worked to eject her, it seemed that they wanted to hurt her, too. Why else would they be driving so slowly?

I had never seen a naked woman before. I was moved to turn away; I was rooted to the spot. The scene was all wrong, a nightmare Wonderland. I thought to myself, *She must be cold.* I saw my mother crying at my side, her face streaked with shiny lines. Hunched over on her knees, in the dark, she looked like a small girl.

As the car cruised past us, the woman lost her equilibrium. Her left leg dragged along the asphalt, a sound to make you cringe. It was all too savage and intense. Five houses down, after a particularly cruel punch, she yielded and fell tumbling to the street. The car roared off.

The woman rose to her feet, her skin a map of raw abrasions. Incredibly, she ran down the block, imploring the men to return. Was she *crazy?* Was she trying to get her dress back? Why would anyone want to be with such brutal people?

"I don't know, Johnny." For once my mother had no answers.

I tried to lean out the window to see what happened next, but my mother tugged me away. Her face was pale, her legs wobbly as we felt our way out of my room and closed the door. I'd stay in my parents' bed that night, as far from the street as possible. I laid down a sheet of newsprint, in case I had an accident, and found my mother's arms. We held each other tight into sleep.

God knows I needed the reassurance, the physical certainty that my mother was all right. More and more it appeared that the world belonged to mean-hearted men. The obscene picture lodged behind my eyelids, unbidden, indelible: the sad, scraped body jettisoned to the street, tossed off like a beer bottle. I'd imagine her swiveling toward me, to scream one more time, but with a difference that stole my sleep that night and for many to come.

Now I knew who she was.

Now she wore my mother's face.

A Gates Avenue fantasy . . .
First the smashing of the cheap outer door. The footsteps creaking on the stairway, each one a little louder, a little closer. Our doorknob rattling impatiently. (The lock is a flimsy thing, and I know it won't hold for long.)

The room is dark and shadowy. I look to my mother. She is wide-eyed, frozen with fear. We can't afford a telephone; there is no one who can help us. There is only a

pretty twenty-nine-year-old woman and her Johnny Boy
with his big head and spindly arms.

I've seen the way young men leer at her when we pass
them on the sidewalk. I've watched how they treat their
own girlfriends. I cannot let a man like that come in here.
With newfound strength, I push our chest of drawers
against the door.

The rattling stops; the pounding begins. The chest
shudders with each blow. I hear the man outside grunt-
ing. He sounds really mad and really strong. I see a slit of
light where the door has cracked ajar.

I stand in my white boxers and T-shirt, between the
door and my mother, steeling myself for the worst. The
slit widens. I think, *If it gets really bad, I'll do something.*
But how can I fend off a grown man?

Still, I am responsible. I must save my mother. I must
do *something* . . .

I grew up with the clacking of trains. One block beyond Ralph Avenue, the BMT line ran elevated over the
dusky bazaar of Brooklyn's Broadway, a negative print of
the Great White Way. Broadway divided our neighborhood from Bushwick, an enclave of second-generation
Italians and Poles. The shops there were our DMZ, the
place where black and white crossed paths.

When I went out with my mother Saturday mornings,
the trip's highlight was a nearby pork store. She liked the
place because it was so clean, with sawdust on the floor
and starched white coats and caps on the butchers. I
liked it for the pungent aromas and the man with the
thick German accent: "Oh *ja,* he's a good boy, isn't he,
Mrs. Johnson?" He'd look down at me and say, "You want
a piece of wurst?"

I'd nod, shy and ravenous, as the butcher sliced off a
chunk of knockwurst. He'd lean over the counter—he
had a dark, wide mustache and massive arms—and drop

the treasure in my hand. As I got bigger, so did the chunks. They symbolized my first friendly encounters with white people.

(Not every merchant was so welcoming. I once trailed my mother into a fabric store to return some defective yarn. A sallow man behind the register waved his hand and said brusquely, "No exchanges—this ain't Macy's." When my mother persisted, the man shoved us out the door.)

For a snack my father might take us to the local Nedick's. Once he got so busy scolding me that he reached for the wrong metal-topped dispenser, and poured sugar on his hot dog instead of mustard. "God *damn* it!" he yelled, waving the ruined frank at me as if I'd steered him wrong. My father was easily discombobulated, and now he stamped his feet, berating the fates. My mother and I giggled helplessly. It was a wonder he didn't sock me there in public.

On Saturday afternoons I'd meet my school friends at the Monroe Theater, where twelve cents bought a triple feature, a serial, and twenty-one cartoons. On Sundays my mother took me to an "art house" downtown or to the first-run theaters on Broadway, either the RKO Bushwick, an ornate stone edifice that now houses a bank, or the Loew's near the subway station, which we knew as "Lowey's." These required more of an investment: a quarter a head, plus a nickel for my beloved Caramello bar.

When it came to movies, my mother and I were omnivorous. *Double Indemnity, Casablanca, Bringing Up Baby, Red River*—we devoured them all. I revered Katharine Hepburn and the more natural actors like Glenn Ford and Humphrey Bogart. My favorite was Tyrone Power, for his casual good looks and intelligence. He always seemed relaxed, even in souped-up swashbucklers like *Captain From Castile.*

But the film that moved me most had nary a swordfight nor a laugh line. *The Red Shoes* hooked me with the liquid beauty of ballet and Moira Shearer's flashing legs and flaming hair. What suspense! Would the ballerina stay with the dashing opera composer? (They were so in love.) Or would she be pulled back to dance by the tyrannical impresario? Romance or duty? Passion or art?

I got lost in that movie, simply taken away. I rooted for the composer, of course, though I sensed that Moira's dilemma had no neat solution. When she leapt to her poignant death (what *was* it about those ballet dancers?), I was crushed. I'd lost track of my mother, who was dabbing at her face with her handkerchief. Outside the theater I felt disjointed by the light, rudely shaken awake.

The Red Shoes embodied all that I yearned for: a life in far-flung places, creating great works. I wanted to feel the things felt by Moira and her lover. I was a ten-year-old boy from Brooklyn and I was longing to be leveled by love, wasted by love, with Paris or Monte Carlo as the backdrop.

In her own way, I think, my mother was drawing me a roadmap out of Bed-Stuy. She made me an unexpected present, a hardcover dictionary, *Funk & Wagnalls New College Standard*. The first blank page carried words in her flowing hand:

> *To John E. Johnson Jr.*
> *February 1949*
> *From Mother & Dad*

As the fattest book I'd ever opened, jammed with dense type and miniature illustrations, the dictionary intrigued me. It also puzzled me, because I knew it had to be expensive and my birthday lay four months off. It would seem an odd sort of gift until I was much older,

when I could read between the lines of my mother's inscription:

Words are important . . .
   Be smart . . .
        Succeed . . .
            Escape.

In fact, I was doing well at school. I'd taken my counselor's urgings to heart, especially as to my diction. I
didn't want to sound like the neighborhood kids, and
Mrs. Purvis made it okay to be different. My speech teachers? Errol Flynn and Cary Grant were too British, but
Spencer Tracy was good, and Tyrone Power ideal: clear
yet unaffected, with no discernible accent.

Years later, when I began talking for a living, people
wondered where I'd been raised. They had no way of
guessing New York, much less inner-city Brooklyn, because my models were all-American movie stars.

On weekdays, restricted to radio, I'd imitate actors on
The FBI in Peace and War, Jack Armstrong, and, first and
last, *The Lone Ranger.* With due respect to Clayton
Moore, there was no matching the Ranger's radio voice,
a forgotten genius named Brace Beemer. He was a bass-
baritone with Wagnerian pipes; crank up the volume and
he'd make the water glasses hum.

After the show was over and I went to bed, I'd parrot
swatches of dialogue learned in one take. I'd fall asleep
doing the Lone Ranger and Tonto and Dan, and also Silver and Scout, the real stars of the show. I nickered and
snorted with verisimilitude, and produced the most life-
like gallop (a trick with my tongue and the roof of my
mouth) east of the King Ranch.

To my mind, a stallion was nature's noblest creature,
the purest expression of freedom and speed. I went to
every classic movie with a horse, from *My Friend Flicka*

to *National Velvet,* if only to see the animals move. (Elizabeth Taylor was a cute little girl, to be sure, but I had eyes only for Pie, the nag they'd entered in the big steeplechase.) I spent hours drawing horses in softbound pads with lined paper, or on the cardboard panels from my father's laundered shirts. I even penned an ode in their honor:

> *There on the block he stood, watching over his*
>   *herd.*
> *Like an unmovable rock he stood, watching every*
>   *movement that occurred.*
> *And when the sun went down, he is silhouetted*
>   *against the sky.*
> *A great black stallion is he . . .*

One day my mother surprised me with a box of tempera paints. Handing me a small brush with a large flourish, she said, "Now you can be a real artist."

It was marvelous to own those bottles of vivid color. But what to use for a surface? The paint soaked through my cheap paper, and canvas board was too pricey for everyday work. I was stymied, left staring at my bare bedroom walls. At last it came to me: I'd *paint* those walls.

With my mother's blessing, I set to work on my little Lascaux. I would paint horses and only horses; anything else seemed a waste of real estate. For inspiration I drew from a potluck of movie Westerns, dime-store novels, and Uncle Syl's quizzes.

Q. Who was the only horse to beat Man O'War?
A. Upset!

I began with pencil drawings and filled in with tempera. While I aimed to match the grandeur of the trompe l'oeil mural, it was hard to sustain a long line. My largest sketches stretched barely a foot, nose to tail. The smaller scale permitted lots of horses—a good thing, as I wanted to leave no one out. Silver and Scout were no-brainers, along with Roy Rogers's Trigger and Gene Autry's Champion, and the Albino, a pink-nosed cinema villain. I painted War Admiral and his archrival Seabiscuit, who beat the son of Man O'War in their mythic match race. I painted every horse I'd ever heard of, from Marengo (Napoleon's mount) to Traveller (Robert E. Lee's). Then I added imaginary steeds: palominos and chestnuts, blacks and Appaloosas, mustangs and pintos and—when space got tight—Shetland ponies.

The most difficult was the rearing white stallion at the center of *The Horse Fair.* Try as I might, I couldn't quite capture the beast's wild spirit.

After my stock of tempera ran dry, I tapped my soda bottle savings to buy more. I lay on my stomach to paint above the baseboard. I stretched on my toes to reach as high as I could, like Michelangelo without the scaffolding. By the time I finished, months later, I'd filled two walls. I went to sleep with herds around me. I felt corralled with them, and less fearful.

My mother was a canny woman. She knew that I needed a safe outlet, even if it strained our meager budget or got her in Dutch with the landlord. She wouldn't shush me when I neighed madly into the night, though I must have driven her bonkers in that shoebox apartment. She allowed me my fantasies; she allowed me to find myself.

Armed with new confidence, I entered a citywide "Clean the Subway" poster contest through my school. My entry halved a subway platform into a "before" (dirty garbage can, rubble littered all around) and an "after" (squeaky-clean can with a smiling face, not a speck of trash in sight).

The next thing I knew, the principal was telling me that I'd won: a big, big deal. They put my name in the

Brooklyn Eagle and plastered my poster on the trains. I was famous; I found it intoxicating.

Mrs. Purvis was delighted, and my mother and aunt made a big to-do, but my father hardly seemed to notice. He paid considerably more attention when I painted his vintage Lionel train set, the cherished cars he took out at Christmastime. They were nicked and scratched and in need of some sprucing up, I thought. I coated the tempera with shellac, to make it permanent.

When my father saw my handiwork, he was too hurt to be mad. He gaped at me and kept repeating, "How could you possibly do this?" I guess I'd gone out of control, like Harold with the purple crayon.

Art lent me an identity; I believe that it saved me. For the first time I knew what I wanted to do when I grew up, à la Gene Autry, but with a twist.

I wanted to be the first painting cowboy.

There is a photograph of Little Johnny Boy, age three, taken by my mother with her box camera. In my hooded snowsuit, I've struck a classic fight pose: left foot pointed forward, weight back, left hand poised to throw a jab. My face is grave, as if to say, *I'm not here to have fun. This is serious business.*

Going back to my Grandfather Johnson, the champ's drinking buddy, my father grew up as a boxing fan. As a young man he'd work out in a gym, and he started me younger still. In boxing he was my true mentor: savvy, reliable, exacting but patient.

His earliest lessons consisted of raising his hands, palms out, and exhorting me to strike them in the classic combination: *Okay, give me a jab, give me a jab, give me a right* . . . I'd never really looked at my father's hands before, and I was amazed at how large they were. They had long and furrowed lifelines, like a map of the Amazon River.

When I got older, maybe six or seven, we'd spar a bit whenever he came home feeling good. Move and bop, push and shove, dance around—lots of fun. By my tenth year he was polishing my footwork and drumming his core principle: "You've got to be able to jab, Johnny. Your jab sets up everything else." He belittled pro boxers who mincingly flicked their left hands. If a jab was strong enough, he'd note, it could stun the opponent and set up your right cross. My father's benchmark was Joe Louis, whose jab could knock a man down, the equivalent of bunting for a home run.

My father would hold my hand and guide it, coaching me every centimeter of the way: "Turn your body, turn into it now. Get your shoulder behind it and reach, and remember, you've got to *pop* the jab. Your hand is like the end of a whip. You can beat a man with a jab—*bang!*" When he demonstrated, I was impressed; he was a lanky six-footer with an excellent left jab.

Those were the times when my father seemed happiest with me. I burned to win his compliments, which came freely for a change. "Good!" he'd say, laughing, as I buried my fist in his palm. "That's real good!" Boxing was his turf, where he could be strong and generous. It was our chance for physical closeness with no threat attached.

My lessons did not neglect tactics. "When you throw a punch, you better hit something," my father told me. "Don't waste your energy, make it count. Don't miss 'em, *hit* 'em. If you can't hit 'em on the jaw, hit 'em on the arm or on the kneecap. But hit *something*. The best defense is a good offense."

Never let anyone hurt you first, he stressed. Protect yourself. Don't be knocked off your feet—God, don't go down.

I took his point. Winning was lots better than losing

when your body was on the line. I'd learned that much at Daddy's knee.

Fathers want to instill a code of honor in their sons, a way of carrying themselves in the world, and mine was no exception. In his book you didn't run from a one-on-one confrontation. "But if there's too many people," he'd add, "it's better to run and fight another day."

That, as I'd find in my looming adolescence, would be one of his sager pieces of advice.

I made my friends at school. I didn't mess around with the knuckleheads on Gates Avenue, several of them known gang members. There were the Chaplains, who were bad, bad people, pitiless and sadistic, and the El Quintos, who were worse. Rumor had it that the El Quintos hung a teenager in Halsey Street Park. I knew for a fact that they'd beaten some kids with baseball bats, and once shot a Chaplain with a zip gun. The neighborhood wasn't so scandalized by the killing, but even the hard guys shook their heads after the El Quintos crashed the funeral, knives drawn, and set off a new melee.

I blanched at these stories. I grew adept at gang sightings, particularly at Madison Street Park, where the blacktop served as our ball field. Stickball was huge in those days, and we played for keeps. We pitched the Spaldeen on the fly, rather than bounce it, and you had to be handy with your broomstick to slam it to Monroe Street for a homer. Though I lacked size and power, I took pride in my switch-hitting and more than held my own.

The trick was to focus on the action while keeping tabs on the gate in the fence: one way in and one way out. If you saw some gang guys coming, you'd need time to run outside before they cut you off. Otherwise you'd have to scale the high fence to get away.

One day my side was at the plate and I'd let another kid use my new glove in the field. (You didn't really need a glove for stickball, but my father thought it was something a boy should have.) *Cheese it! The El Quintos!* We scattered out the gate. The kid ran away with my mitt, forgotten in my flight.

When I got home, my father was fit to be tied. He took me back to the park, but we found neither kid nor glove.

In those days I went everywhere on the run. I ran to the park and to the movies. I ran to stores and back on errands for my mother, holding hero loaves like relay sticks. My stringy body finally caught up with my big head, and I could *move.* At field day I was the fastest kid at P.S. 70, which meant something.

When I lacked a nickel for the trolley, or the weather was too nice to ride, I'd run home from school along Patchen Avenue. Halfway there I'd near Hancock Street, where some kids had it in for the Gates Avenue crowd, and the chase was on. Normally I'd get a good head start, so it wouldn't be too hairy. But once I was distracted and my pursuers closed to a few yards.

That was when I found a new gear. I was running as absolutely fast as I could, from fear and adrenaline at first, then for the joy of it. The wind whistled by my ears. My feet barely touched down. I was bound for another country, and the boys behind me had no visa. Three blocks later, a backward glance confirmed what I already knew. The Hancock crew had given up. They were off the screen.

You cannot catch what you cannot see.

The amazing thing about Coney Island was that you stepped out of an everyday subway car and into an urban Disneyland. Though past its peak in 1949, it was still *the* great amusement park. I held my parents' hands as we beheld the dreamscape of Steeplechase Park, a gaudy acreage of thrills.

My father was in an expansive mood that day. He

treated me to my first Nathan's hot dog, by far the best I'd ever tasted, and to a hamburger with French fries. He wasn't even fazed when he failed to ring the bell with the sledgehammer. With his second dud he pronounced the game fixed and I believed him, despite the next man's success.

We were fine till he decided to tackle the Cyclone, the *Tyrannosaurus rex* of roller coasters, a twisting figure-eight that rose to eighty-five feet above sea level. I had a mortal fear of heights—I'd get queasy over the Triboro Bridge—and began to whimper, *I don't want to go, I'm scared Daddy, please don't make me go* . . .

My father said, "No, you've *got* to go. This is a great ride, Johnny. This is *fun.* You'll love it, everybody does."

My mother was less enthralled, but my father was a bulldog when he wanted his way, and she didn't feel like arguing. Too soon we were climbing into our car, with me in the middle. The attendants locked the bar down with an ominous thud. I could feel my heart beating as we climbed, up and up, impossibly high, till I had to shut my eyes. We were still rising when I sneaked one last peek at of the ocean below.

Bad timing on my part, because the world picked that moment *to fall away*. We were plummeting down the rails at a million miles an hour, and my stomach did a tango with my small intestine, and I was absolutely certain that my number was up—

"Scream!" my father screamed, over the coaster's roar. "You got to *scream!*"

I opened my mouth but nothing came out. My spine had turned to marmalade. I was too damn scared to scream.

Off the first drop we swooped into a dead man's curve. The centrifugal force crushed my father against my rib cage; I was the tuna fish in the sandwich, and the sandwich was in a vise. That's how it went on my first and last trip on the Cyclone: up and down and whipped around, in an alternating current of pain and nausea. No ride should have lasted as long as that one. No boy could have prayed more fervently for the finish line.

And *boom,* it was over.

They brought up the bar and we staggered out. I began to regret my second hot dog. My father nearly fell over laughing, pointing derisively at his wife's wind-blown hair. My mother was really upset. I didn't hear her curse very often, but she had an impressive vocabulary.

To change the subject, my father led us to the bumper cars. *Now you're talking,* I thought. *This is going to be great.* As I was gauged too short to drive, and my father wanted to go solo, I rode with my mother. She had never gotten her driver's license, and now I understood why: She was helpless behind a wheel. We spun into terminal oversteer from the start, and spent the balance of the ride stuck against the spring-loaded boards, facing the wrong way. We were sitting ducks for any macho maniac zipping around the track . . .

Bang! My father had slammed into us head-on, at full speed, throwing his body forward at the last moment for that extra little oomph of impact. It was my first sensation of whiplash, and I can tell you it was very authentic.

"Got you!" he said, deftly swinging away for another lap. My mother stomped on the gas and jerked the steering wheel with white knuckles. We went nowhere. Our necks were on the guillotine—*wham!* Dad bumped us again, in a shower of snapping sparks.

"Lady driver!" he cackled. He was having a high old time.

Hungry for revenge, I begged my mother, "Can't you turn it around?"

"I'm trying, Johnny, I'm—"

Boom! Two white teenagers, joining the fun at our expense. Then another jolt, as my father rammed into them. But he wasn't laughing anymore. He scowled at the interlopers and said, "What the hell are you doing that for? Can't you see they're stuck?"

"Fuck you, mooley," the driver said, in a corruption of the Italian slur.

My father said, "You just stay the hell away from them, you understand?" The electricity sputtered out. We were done.

My father stalked out of the rink, still blustering at our maltreatment. He wasn't being logical, but I was used to that. At the risk of stretching a metaphor, I'd suggest that my youth was one long bumper ride: a baffle of hurt and protection from the same cruelly twisted man.

In sixth grade I was promoted to the top track, taught by Mrs. Purvis. I was madly infatuated. When my teacher walked down the hall in her cotton-candy sweater, I'd hang close for a whiff of her Chanel No. 5. Had anyone ever smelled so good, so razor clean? I'd feel suffocated; I'd want to take it all in and not breathe out.

My goal was to be the smartest kid in the smartest class. In my school photograph, with my fat face and bow tie, I look like some sawed-off fraternity brat. I'm afraid that I became a smug little know-it-all with his arm locked in *sieg heil,* bleating to be called on. There were times when my own mother couldn't stand it. As I blew on about something, she'd interrupt to chide me, "When did you get so uppity?"

When I ran for student council president, I received two votes, one of them my own. Most everyone hated me, and I paid the piper at lunchtime in the schoolyard. I didn't seem very tough; I would have picked on me, too. (At my mother's insistence, I was the only sixth-grader still wearing knickers, though I'd fold them down toward my ankles as soon as I left our apartment.) Provocation was a matter of opinion: "You looking at *me?*" I never came out worse than a draw, but that didn't discourage the next guy.

Until one afternoon, that is, when I took on a boy at least a head taller, a round-faced, beefy kid with a buzz cut and soiled overalls. He bullied me halfway down the block, by the neat row houses where Mrs. Purvis lived. A ring of spectators shadowed us, hemming us in, precluding retreat. When my foe latched me in a headlock and I strained to free myself, we circled in place. The onlookers swam before me, their hoots floating through the air.

It's no accident that so many great fighters are ghetto-bred. When survival is an open question, ruthlessness becomes a virtue. The one rule is to win. Tiring of our dance, his arm cinched around my ears, the big kid leaned heavily on my neck, jamming my forehead down toward the sharpened spike of a low wrought iron fence. I could see the black point, inches away and closing. The pressure on my head intensified. The boy seemed ready and willing to ventilate my cranium.

He had no idea that I had him just where I wanted him.

Like the rest, he'd judged me by my surface. He didn't know that I'd made my separate peace with fear. After my father's onslaughts, I wasn't about to be intimidated by some junior neighborhood sociopath. I could be ruthless, too.

And so I fought for my life. The other boy was stronger, but I owned the higher urgency. My mouth found a finger and I bit down, with feeling. The kid squealed in pain and eased his grip on my head. He tried to shake me off, but I stuck to his digit like a terrier. If I'd had to, I would've bitten the damn thing off.

I straightened up and felt him weakening. With his finger still between my bicuspids, I hooked a right hand to his mouth. He fell and I fell on top of him, altogether out of my skull. I worked on his face until I felt no more resistance, and then I worked some more, until someone pulled me off.

The story got back to the schoolyard before I did. It was a big fight, Sonny redux, and everybody was stunned that I'd won. I was a made man, no more to be trifled with, and people stayed out of my way.

CHAPTER FIVE

MY GRAMMAR SCHOOL FED INTO J.H.S. 135, A LAUNCH PAD FOR truants and dropouts, a place where futures were foreshortened. At the beginning of sixth grade, though, we were told that a few of us—the best and the brightest—would be plucked out and whisked off to Halsey Junior High, the white school across Broadway in Bushwick. The chosen ones would be among the first black kids to go there.

I put pedal to the metal that year. I was determined to get into Halsey, not for the sake of integration or to be a pioneer, but simply because it was better. It was the place for smart kids, and I knew I was too smart to stay in Bedford-Stuyvesant.

On the last day of school, Mrs. Purvis gave out our grades and faced us with her lovely smile. "These report cards really mattered this year," she said. "Here are the children who are going to 135." She read off a couple dozen names. "And here are the children going to Halsey." That list was much shorter.

There were some high-powered people in my sixth-grade class. Philip Taylor became an orthopedic surgeon; Sanford Allen would play first violin with the New York

Philharmonic. But I was the one boy picked to go to Halsey—*yes!* It was my first baby step toward a different life.

On the opening day of seventh grade, I peeped around my homeroom like a turtle from its shell. As the only black kid in the top track, I felt keyed up and a little scared. When the teacher asked a question in these parts, *everybody* raised a hand.

But my butterflies soon subsided. I came from a household where great books were read for entertainment. My mother consumed three or four newspapers a day, cover to cover, including the *New York Herald Tribune.* After years of Uncle Syl's quizzes, I could have been impaneled on *Meet the Press.*

I was ready, in short, for a challenge. My worry was that I'd *look* inferior because I was so poor. At lunchtime I found an ally in Willie Kinard, another threadbare pilgrim from Bed-Stuy. Willie was tall and skinny, a crackerjack at math and a man of the world. Where I had been sheltered, he was wise to the ways of girls. He taught me how to fill out a slang book and kept me current on the latest grind-me-up, the sort of party I'd never been to, where the lights were low and you danced real close.

The Bushwick kids lived on another planet, or so it had seemed to me, but the ones in my class were open and friendly. Soon I was riding the bus with people named Craig Nardine and Joseph Conigliaro, or walking down Bushwick Avenue toward their fancy buildings.

I was walking as well with a ponytailed madonna named Theresa Sant. *Theresa Sant*—had there ever been a girl so exquisite? She had clear olive skin and strong, expressive brows. She wore saddle shoes and ankle socks, and she was so pretty. The first time I saw her in homeroom, I had that empty-pit sensation in my stomach, that blood rush to the surface of my skin. I felt different than with Mrs. Purvis: more self-conscious, more alive. From that first day I was in love.

Craig and Joseph and Theresa and the rest became my peer group through three years at Halsey. We were inseparable until late afternoon, when I'd board the Broadway bus back to Gates Avenue. I began to live a bifurcated life, though Joseph once came to my house to see my horse murals.

Socially, the honors kids were squares like myself. My mother wouldn't let me out past dark, which took care of sex or drugs or even a guilty Schlitz. I was an innocent, a lamb. But I didn't mind as long as Theresa smiled at me each morning.

Early in the term, when it was still warm outside, Joseph Conigliaro asked me to stay after school for a game of handball. I was reluctant at first. I'd already been shoved once or twice by the "greasers," the kids who ruled shop class and terrorized the hallways, and I knew they hung out by the playground. But I hadn't had any real trouble. I assumed that the greasers didn't like me because I was one of the smart kids. I was used to that, so I told Joseph okay.

Like my father, I had not learned my place.

We'd played a handful of points when a basketball rolled onto our court. It was followed by half a dozen ninth-graders with bad skin and low foreheads. The leader of the pack walked up to me and snarled, "What the fuck are *you* doing here?" He had on chartreuse pegged pants and black shoes, a fashion statement I'd remember, as I'd be spending some quality time at his shin level.

I said to myself, *This is going to be trouble.* I glanced at Joseph and thought, *Did he set me up?*

By then the question was moot, because I'd broken my father's cardinal rule; I was flat on the ground. Two greasers held me down while the leader wound up and hurled the basketball at my face. I turned my neck just in time—the ball bounced off the side of my head, which was painful enough. More angry-looking people gathered around. Joseph was nowhere to be seen. I felt the first kick and coiled against those to come.

I'd been hearing a ragged chorus without listening, but now the voices fell into focus: *Nigger! Nigger! You no-good black nigger!*

It may sound naive, but the name-calling hurt most of all. I was acquainted with the ultimate American obscenity; I'd heard Mama Tutt use it on my father often enough. But I'd never heard it used this way, with such raving hatred, by people who seemed set upon ending me.

Pulled to my feet, I took my chance to look around. What I saw was alarming: a sea of white people. Not just Halsey students, but full-grown men who loitered after school let out, plus a healthy turnout of their ladies' auxiliary, all swarming to get their licks in. *Jesus Christ,* I thought, *are the grandmothers going to come and beat me, too?*

I began clicking in and out: sound, no sound; sound, no sound. As the crowd rained its punches, I steeled myself not to lose consciousness. The interesting part is that I kept my cool. *Think on your feet, Johnny, think on your feet. What's your next move? How can you get away?*

It dawned on me why they'd let me up; they'd devised a new game. The men took me to the top of the concrete steps. They hoisted me over the edge, till my feet were dangling, then heaved me headfirst to the bottom, where others waited. I was fortunate to get my arms out in front of my fall.

The men who'd thrown me came down to drag me back up again. It wasn't hard to glean their pattern. They would beat me until they had *beaten* me. They would throw me till I broke.

But now I knew what was coming. As I tumbled to the bottom a second time, I took my sprinter's crouch. Slipping free from a knot of sweaty arms, I shot out of the schoolyard. My jaw throbbed, my ribs grabbed. My thighs burned with each stride. But I shut out the pain and kept moving. I could hear the wolves baying their expletives. I could not afford to be run down.

I cut a hard right on Evergreen past the front of the school, with a flash of chartreuse hot behind me. I hooked left on Halsey Street, a beeline to Bed-Stuy, where I knew they wouldn't follow. I didn't look back. I flew past Broadway and Saratoga Park, a favored haunt of the El Quintos. I'd had enough excitement for one day.

My mother winced at the sight of my face. While I didn't cry, I was sincerely rattled. "I'm not going back there," I said. "Those people are crazy."

She got that pig iron look in her eye and said, "Yes, you are going back to that goddamn school, and you are going back tomorrow." She was a stubborn woman when it came to her only child. She knew that quitting was addictive, and wasn't about to let me start.

"But you can't fight all those hoodlums yourself," she went on. "The school has to do something." The next morning, my parents took me to the principal's office and lodged a complaint, which I knew would be no use. A few hours later, when I passed the greasers in the corridor, they laughed at me—*laughed* at me! I promised myself that I'd get even, somehow.

Over the next few weeks, come the final bell, I made sure to be the first one off school grounds. Otherwise, life went on. I never seriously mulled a transfer to a lesser school in Bed-Stuy. For me there could be no turning back.

While I nursed a grudge toward my attackers (and got some small revenge two years later, when I caught one of them alone), I never thought to impugn white people en masse. I decided that Joseph was blameless; I trusted my new friends.

And I still loved Theresa. The following year, after I'd shed my caution, a group of us got up a round of punchball after school. Theresa shivered in the autumn cool and asked to borrow my jacket. I tried to be casual as I helped her slip it on, but my soul was winging to the sky. There were other jackets she might have borrowed and plenty of other boys who liked her. She was making a statement, and she knew it.

How smitten was I? I would willingly have been beaten every day for the privilege of attending Halsey Junior High School and gazing at Theresa Sant.

Our Polaroid moments were few. I remember a class party at Christmastime, when I held mistletoe over Theresa and kissed her on the cheek, and thought I would collapse because she smelled so good. I can recall, as if it were last week, the time she came to my block with two other kids for cover. The group of us ambled down Gates Avenue to a candy store on Broadway, and we laughed and laughed. It was nothing special at all. It was one of the incandescent days of my life.

But that was as far as it went. Theresa never set foot in my apartment. There was no way for us to be together, not in 1951. Our friends all knew how I felt, and why I never had a girlfriend in junior high school, but we didn't discuss it openly. Interracial dating might fly for a musician like Uncle Manzie or Syl's bohemian friends in Greenwich Village. But for a boy from Bedford-Stuyvesant and a girl from Bushwick, it was a nonnegotiable taboo. Theresa would be ostracized; I might be killed.

One Saturday I stopped at the Broadway pork store and ran into Theresa with her mother. Though she said hello and introduced me, she was shy and a little distant.

I understood perfectly, even as her coolness cut me to the quick.

But I still loved Theresa Sant. There remains a place in my heart for her to this day.

After we'd moved to Brooklyn, my father bought a dull green Hudson Hornet, a fifty-dollar rattletrap that had seen better decades. We used it to visit our relatives in Harlem, or on pleasure trips to the beaches on Long Island. The Hornet badly needed a ring job, and we had to keep a can of oil in the trunk, but it got us where we wanted to go.

Befitting a former cabbie, my father was smart and aggressive at the wheel. As I watched him, bug-eyed, it came to me that driving was man's work. My mother was disinclined to get her license even before our bumper car fiasco. When my father gave her a lesson, she'd get ruffled. "Irene can't drive," he would say, as if stating the Pythagorean theorem. "Your mama gets too upset."

And my mother would say, "That's right, I don't have the patience for it."

If my father was ever to get spelled at the wheel, or to hand off the keys after drinking, there was only one candidate: *moi*. The fact that I was twelve years old was a mere technicality.

One day we pulled into an Amoco station and my father got out to check the oil. When he asked my mother to pull the hood latch, she released the hand brake instead. As the Hornet began rolling into busy Bushwick Avenue, she froze at the switch. Not thinking twice, I dove forward from the rear seat. With my legs in the air, my knees straddling the front bench, I yanked the emergency brake and pushed down on the foot brake with my hand for good measure.

Impressed by my sangfroid, my father decided that my time had come. We began practicing after school, before his graveyard shift at the post office, while my mother worked as a matron at United Cerebral Palsy. "The first thing," he told me solemnly, "is that you have to pay attention. This is a big machine, and a little mistake can give you a big problem."

Over the next few weeks, he put me through the basics: shifting from first into reverse, backing up, parking on the right, parking on the left. My dad was a great instructor, always calm, never raising his voice. If I hesitated, he'd say, "Be decisive. If you're going to make a move, *make* it."

One day he took me uptown by St. James Church, where the street banked on a steep incline. He stopped the car pointing uphill and said, "A good driver can get into gear on a hill without rolling back. If you do it just right, you don't even need the brake. You can hold the car right there between the clutch and the gas, and feel your way into first gear. That's when you have real control."

He showed how, then switched seats with me. I promptly stalled and slammed on the brake. My father said, "That's all right, you just let up too quick on the clutch." His assurance was infectious. By my third try, I had the hill licked.

I looked forward to our practice sessions. Along with the afternoon breakfasts I'd cook for him, and our impassioned talks about sports, they colored our days together. We had an easy rapport on the road, my father and I. It was more relaxed between us when my mother wasn't there.

My maiden run to the city came on a Saturday night, when the three of us set off to dinner in Harlem. My father opened the driver's door and said, "Can you do this?"

I said, "Yeah, I can do it." I tried to sound matter-of-fact, but I was quaking inside. This would be way better than the Cyclone.

As I settled behind the wheel, all five-foot-four of me, my mother made some anxious noises. But my father calmed her—"He'll be fine, Irene, this boy can *drive*"— and then he turned to me and said grandly, as though I were a liveried chauffeur, "Take us to Manhattan!"

I can hardly describe the effect of my dad's command. In that instant, my sense of self was made over. I became the most able, precocious, improbably clever boy in the borough of Brooklyn. My father was so hard to please that I'd nearly stopped trying, but I could not fool myself. I still curried his favor. I still longed for his praise and approval, his meaty pat on my back.

I took hold of the wheel and checked my mirrors, and stretched my legs to reach the pedals. Then, screened from cops by the darkness, I took my parents to Manhattan: down Gates to Bushwick Avenue and out toward Cemetery of the Evergreens, where we entered the tricky business of the evening, the Interboro Parkway. Since renamed for Jackie Robinson, the Interboro was a narrow, twisting road, full of shoulderless stretches and hairpin bends, divided by a concrete retaining wall. It was densely used, with numerous merges. At any number of points—a sharp right at an underpass near the Van Wyck Expressway, another onto the Grand Central, where a careless motorist might cut you off at full speed—there was no room for error.

I relished every mile of it; I *loved* driving. I loved the engine's throaty voice, and how I could change its tune with a tap on the accelerator. (I envisioned a nest of sliding valves and cylinders under the hood, like the works in Chaplin's *Modern Times*.) I loved how my slightest nudge of the steering wheel was conveyed to the bigger wheels outside. I tracked the play of taillights like an air traffic controller. The thought of an error, a crash, never crossed my mind. I was completely in charge of things.

Every so often my father would murmur his assent or

cast a satisfied rearward glance at my mother. His protégé was passing the road test with flying colors. Junior had the right stuff, and hadn't he known it all along?

When I remember that ride, it seems like the strangest thing. My father was so full of contradiction. On the one hand, he had great faith in me, to where he'd trust me with his life when I was barely out of knickers.

Then he'd turn on a dime, blind and reckless, and take an axe to the small ego he'd built. Just like that, in a wink, I'd lay in splinters.

Toward the end of seventh grade, a Jamaican woman bought our building. She evicted our menacing neighbors and gave notice that her daughter was taking our apartment. If we wanted to stay, we'd have to move to the back room.

Deprivation, as an absolute fact, is not the most ruinous part of poverty. It's the knowing that your life can get *worse,* without warning, and there isn't a blessed thing you can do about it.

I lost my herds of horses, soon to be painted over, along with the pencil-scratched journal on my windowsill. My masterpiece and my history, gone in one swoop. I'd move my sporadic diary, and its sugarplum tributes to my parents, to the blank sheets of my Funk & Wagnalls. But it wouldn't be the same.

When you have just a little and lose it, it can hurt more than losing a lot.

I slept on our pullout sofa in the "living area," a few steps from my parents' alcove. Our room opened onto the hallway by the shared bath and kitchen, where it was noisy all the time. We were three rats in a cage again, and it wouldn't be long before Papa Rat bit someone's head off.

I was under pressure all the time. At school, where the handful of Bed-Stuy émigrés worked under a spotlight, I had to succeed—to show that I could compete, but mainly to feed my parents' aspirations. A college degree would be my passport to a better life. The standard question—*How are you doing in school?*—was semi-rhetorical in my family, with only one answer: *I'm doing good.*

That spring my mother and I met with my guidance counselor, a coiffed platinum blonde who dripped with too much of everything: big earrings, painted lips, neatly filed cherry claws. She spoke to us slowly, drawing out her vowels to make sure that my mother understood. Overlooking my grades, she suggested that I point toward a trade school: "Your people do very well in auto mechanics, for example."

My mother was incensed. "Why should he do that?" she said. "He has a very high IQ." The counselor checked her manicure. The conference was over.

"She's just an old prejudiced person," said my mother, fuming all the way home. "You go ahead and do your work."

I'd bring my report card to my father as soon as he woke up. He'd look it up and down as I stood there by his bed like a West Point plebe on review. If he was in a good humor, he might grunt and hand it back to me. If he was cranky (the norm), I'd get the third degree. "What's this 85?" he'd say. "Why didn't you do better in math?"

By the latter part of junior high, I was fed up. What did he know, anyway? He'd never gone to school with white kids or gotten marks to match mine. For years I'd watched him practice for the postal exam, sorting index cards into cardboard compartments, and he'd yet to score high enough for a permanent job. Meanwhile, I was making the honor roll. I was doing my best; I didn't need to be badgered.

Finally I said, "What did *you* get in math?"

It was my first blurt of rebellion, and my father took it

badly. He leapt out of bed and growled, "What did you say, boy?"

I backpedaled in a hurry: "I was just wondering what did you get—" Before I could retreat, he smacked me really hard.

He was smacking more often these days, though the ritual whippings were past. His outbursts bewildered me because I did nothing to provoke them. I didn't smoke or steal or get anyone pregnant. I came home at the appointed hour. I toed the line in every way.

Why is he doing this? I'd ponder, as I picked myself off the floor. My father was like a foreign crossword puzzle. I couldn't read the clues, much less solve the damn thing.

After his late shift at the post office, he often joined some co-workers on a seedy stretch of 34th Street, where sex shows and hookers plied the morning trade. When he finally came home, toward noon, he'd be sour and testy.

I'd be long gone, barring a school holiday. Then it would be just me and my dad and his day-after smell in one room. Once he told me to make him some scrambled eggs and toast, and I hopped to it. He was in a wicked mood, not to be kept waiting.

At thirteen I was a capable short-order cook, but this once I forgot to line the pan with butter. The eggs stuck to the bottom, burnt beyond redemption, and we had no more for a second try. I knew that I'd made an unforgivable mistake.

When my father heard me scraping the pan into the garbage, he looked up and said, "What happened?"

I said, "I messed up the eggs." He was quiet then. A viper plays no overtures.

Hanging my head, I followed him back to our apartment. He said, "Bring me a glass of water." I returned to the kitchen, drew the water, returned to our room, and stood there apprehensively. My father was busy with something; I took a nervous gulp from the glass. When he finally grabbed it, he said, "That's not a full glass of water, that's a half glass of water. Can't you do *anything* right?"

I said, stammering, "I didn't know you wanted a full one."

"You must be really stupid," he said. And then he swung, with the glass still in his hand: a right to the side of my face, smooth and rhythmic, with a nice weight shift. I dropped like a stone and nearly went out; my father outweighed me by a hundred pounds. As I took my ten-count, I saw his mouth contorting angrily, and I realized that I'd lost the audio portion of our program. *I can't hear—I can't hear!* It was fright more than pain that drove me to tears.

"Stop crying!" my father roared in a faraway voice. *"Stop-your-damn-crying!"* I think he'd hit me so hard that it scared him.

I heard nothing out of my left ear for the rest of that day, and the ringing lasted nearly a week. I worried that the damage might be permanent, but I didn't complain. I would not give him that satisfaction.

In typing class, where I was all thumbs at the keyboard, I sat and daydreamed. I revisited the sequence of events: eggs, water, haymaker. What galled me was that I knew I might have blocked it; I had seen the swing coming and could have thrown up my arm in time. But I'd squelched the reflex in accordance with our rules. Any defense would launch my father into a spiral of mayhem. What began as punishment would end in combat, with only one possible victor.

I had to submit to him, like it or not. I had to take my dive and hope that I would not drown.

At bedtime my mother and I advanced from Mark Twain to Melville. I was stirred by Ahab's dark obsession, disturbed by the fate of innocent Billy Budd. When Claggart, the envious master-at-arms, frowned at the sight of poor Billy's spilled soup, I could smell the tragedy coming a mile away. I understood Claggart. I knew implacable evil, boy, and it really frightened me, because I also knew how it could render good helpless.

These men are madmen, Melville wrote, *and of the most dangerous sort, for their lunacy is not continuous, but occasional, evoked by some special object* . . .

Oh, yes, I knew just what he meant.

When the call came through on our new telephone, I could tell the news was bad from the veins in my father's neck. "That son of a bitch!" he said. He slammed down the receiver and shooed me into the Hudson.

My father drove fast all the time, but not this fast. Sputtering curses, he passed on to me what he'd heard: "Emmett and Manzie had a fight, and Emmett bit off your uncle's bottom lip!"

What was I to make of *that?* And what was Daddy planning to do about it?

We squealed to a stop on St. Nicholas Avenue. My father pulled a tire iron from the Hornet's trunk and told me to wait at Aunt Marian's candy store. He tore down the street like a madman, ready to stave Emmett in and avenge Manzie's mutilated profile.

But I knew the real reason my father had come unhinged, and it had nothing to do with my uncle. He was going to kill Emmett because Emmett had been with my mother.

To my relief, my old patron was nowhere to be found. We eventually went home, my father still seething.

Uncle Manzie would claim that he'd been defending my mother's honor—a tough sell, as chivalry wasn't one of his virtues. By next day the story was all over the streets. As I heard it, my uncle had come off a gig and straight into a bar, his set routine. He began to paradiddle but his timing was off, thanks to an ungodly number of rotgut whiskeys.

Emmett looked over and said, "Hell, I can do better than that."

Offended, Manzie said, "I'd like to see you try."

Emmett took the challenge and the drumsticks. He had some real chops, and laid down a beat that got the whole joint jumping. It was no contest. He'd defeated the great Manzie Johnson at his own game.

Chagrined, my uncle must have said something unkind, or maybe he led with his fists. He had no better luck fighting than drumming, though; you have to know that a man who works the streets can take care of himself. Emmett saw his opportunity, chomped down with his even white teeth, and that was that. People said that it could have been worse. Manzie might have been a trumpet player, for example.

Even with his disfigurement, my uncle remained a fine-looking man. He grew a fringe of beard under his missing lip, so it wouldn't be so noticeable. But his run-in with Emmett took some starch out of him. It wasn't long before he traded in his sticks for a chauffeur's cap and settled in the Bronx with Aunt Margie.

While Uncle Manzie still caroused now and then, he was a stallion no longer. He aged badly, lost a lung to TB, and died of cancer in his early sixties.

My father would hound my mother about Emmett for years to come. He might as well have railed against the wind, however, because the numbers man was never seen or heard from again.

CHAPTER SIX

GIVEN MY CHRONIC GUILT (*WHAT KIND OF A BOY HATES HIS father?*), my nagging need for approval, and my gnawing dread of death and whatever came next, you could say I was delivered to the Church on a platter.

In Bedford-Stuyvesant I resumed my instruction at Our Lady of Good Counsel, a stone sanctuary on Putnam Avenue. My mother and I were by-the-book Catholics: fish on Friday, confession on Saturday, mass on Sunday morning. It wasn't a chore for me to go to church. Outside I lived my days in a state of alert, looking out for the next potential threat. But when I knelt amid the Fourteen Stations of the Cross, life slowed down. My angst fell away. All seemed cool and monastic, orderly and clear.

I'd grown into a true believer, though I mostly skirted God-the-father with his Old Testament anger, his big stick for those who crossed him. I prayed instead to the sacrificial son, or to the Virgin Mary, a blameless mother like my own. On Christmas Eve I'd gaze at the crèche by the altar and wish the baby Jesus a happy birthday, out loud.

By seventh grade I'd progressed to confirmation lessons with Brother Donald, an Irish Jesuit out of a Spencer Tracy movie: black hair, robins egg blue eyes,

Mama Tutt

Me at age three-and-a-half with
Grandma Johnson

My grandfather's New York City taxi license

My mom's high school
graduation portrait (1936)

Mom and Dad before they
were married (1935)

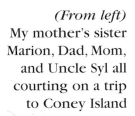

(From left)
My mother's sister
Marion, Dad, Mom,
and Uncle Syl all
courting on a trip
to Coney Island

My dad John, Sr.
at sixteen
months and
twenty-four

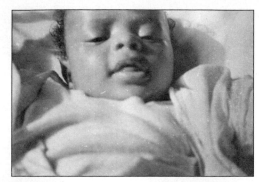

Me at six
weeks

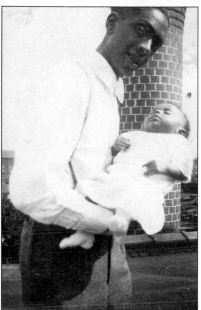

At two months

At eighteen months—
my first pony ride

My high school graduation
portrait (1956)

Happy times with my parents

A day at the Bronx Zoo
with my first son Eric

(From left) Eric, Christine, Cydney, and Anthony (CREDIT: EVELYN FLORET)

Winning my sixth
Emmy

Landing a jab on
Floyd Patterson
(CREDIT: ARLENE
SCHULMAN)

Interviewing President Ford (CREDIT: CAMERA ARTS STUDIO)

In the thick of the Persian Gulf
War on the Iraq-Kuwait border

With André Watts

Interviewing
Sidney Poitier (1968)

and skin so white it was nearly translucent. (After he'd shaved, you could see his veins.) The brother was in his mid-thirties and at first seemed severe; there was no cutting up in confirmation class. Clasping his hands beneath his tunic, he'd pace tigerlike and pop questions at the slack or distracted.

I had never encountered a man like Brother Donald. He was learned yet humble, strong yet exceedingly kind. He represented another marker in my life, one more person who saw something in me and tried to nurture it along.

I won him over with my work ethic. With my mother's help, I learned my catechism front to back and won a clutch of medals, including the coveted St. Christopher's tie clasp. I was absurdly proud of my awards, and bereft when some burglars made off with them.

After class was out, my instructor might walk me home through Madison Street Park. Those were lovely times: two friends strolling and talking of Higher Things, unmindful of the squalor around them. Brother Donald was fond of the essays of Montaigne and the notion of the Renaissance man, the gentleman who could spin a sonnet as well as brandish a rapier. He led me to the intricate theology of St. Thomas Aquinas, my first clue that there might be one Catholicism for the masses and another for intellectuals like the good brother.

My mentor surfaced at a crucial moment, in time to nip my budding cynicism. I'd once trusted that good works led to good things in return, but life had red-penciled me the hard way. How could my dear mother be treated so badly by my father? Where was the fairness in that? How could God allow it?

Before I strayed too far, however, Brother Donald interjected a new concept: goodness for its own sake. "The process is the thing, not the end product," he said. "The reward comes from the inside. Think of it this way—you don't just go to church to ask God for something. You go to be a part of something, to believe in something larger and better than yourself."

In Brother Donald's view, it wasn't enough to confess by the numbers: "You have to get beyond, 'This is good and this is bad.' There's more to religion than that."

"What do you mean?"

"Look, John, you can go and confess the same sin over and over again. But at some point you have to start questioning, 'Why am I doing this sin?' Religion is asking you to look inside yourself, to ask more of yourself.

"For example, why did you work harder than anyone else on your catechism?" (I flashed to my stash of medals and despised my vanity.) "Because when you worked harder, you understood more. If you carry that through, you'll take religion to a higher level."

Harps and brimstone did not enter Brother Donald's equation. He cared about the deeds that made you a better Catholic *today;* he taught me the value of being human. By the end of our first year together, I thought I'd found my calling. I wanted to be a priest.

One day, at the end of our walk, Brother Donald asked to come inside. I wasn't keen on people seeing our cramped apartment, but he insisted. He shook hands with my startled parents, fixed them with his brilliant eyes, and said, "I wanted to meet John's mother and father, because I knew that they must be tremendous people to have such a wonderful young man for a son."

He went on for a while about how smart and sensitive I was. He wasn't rude or presumptuous for a moment, but he'd come with a subtext: *I have recognized John as a remarkable boy, and surely you must know that, too. You need to cherish what is good in him. You need to guard his future.*

My mother was grateful to Brother Donald, but my father seemed put off. He resented the Catholic Church and how it snatched his wife away on weekends. For my father, prayer was a private conversation, a view that conveniently kept him in bed Sunday mornings. He considered himself an expert on Eastern religion—he'd read a few pages of the Bhagavad Gita—and loved to expound upon his Doctrine of the Pinky.

"The pinky is the least important of the fingers," he'd say. "But if it gets infected, it can destroy the whole hand, and the hand can destroy the entire body. The smallest thing can be the most important. The pinky can be a whole universe by itself."

(When my father waxed profound with his in-laws, Mama Tutt dubbed him "The Great Philosopher." Though my mother and I wouldn't risk such frontal sarcasm, we made faces behind his back. Sedition was in the wind.)

As I look back, though, my father's unease with Brother Donald may have had little to do with theology. More likely he was jealous of a man I emulated. Or perhaps he worried that our secret might seep out . . .

Brother Donald left no wiggle room in matters moral. Once I joined some kids at a candy shop where the owner was crippled. One boy bounced his change off the counter, forcing the old man to bend to get it. Before he could straighten up, the others had stuffed their pockets with Mars bars.

I was horrified; I had never stolen in my life. Before assimilating the fear of God, I'd had the fear of Dad to stop me. A sense of rectitude ran deep in my father, who would not so much as cheat on his taxes. He'd say, "If I ever catch you lying or stealing, it's your hide," and I hadn't tested him since the tadpole pond.

Back outside, I told the boys, "You'll be punished for this." They eyed me quizzically before returning to their nougat.

I was no less prudish when it came to pleasures of the flesh. I grew up in a household where such things were not discussed. My mother was an innocent and my father the classic American male, the satyr who got his kicks out of sex being dirty.

I can remember my first rude exposure. I was nine years old, at the Monroe Theater, and some boys passed around a flip book of a man with an enormous penis having inter-course. They said, "That's what your mother and father do!"

Aghast, I insisted they were wrong: "*My* mother doesn't do *that!*"

I kept a mental scoreboard, tabulating sins for my next confession. For a time I had nothing more to report than a few curse words. But in junior high I fell prey to lewd thoughts. The turning point was a Western where my eyes kept straying from the horses to an actress named Debra Paget. I was glued to the curves within the cow-girl's gingham—and what was that stiffening in my lap?

The dam had burst, so to speak, and I was flooded with erotic images. Granted, they were mild by the stan-dards of puberty. All I wanted to do was to kiss Theresa Sant on the lips. But still I was glad that Brother Donald—a righteous bear for respecting women—wasn't privy to the booth.

After receiving the magic number of Our Fathers and Hail Marys, I'd kneel at the altar rail for my penance. On Saturdays the church would be quiet and softly lit, and my mind would wander. I'd lose count and start over, be-cause you could not fool God. I remember my day of in-famy, when I'd missed church three weeks running and was dunned two sets of twenty. I was at the rail forever, as less grievous sinners came and went, came and went. They must have made me for a double homicide, or at least some wanton masturbation.

I felt cleansed by each confession, bound to do better. When my mother and I went to mass the next day, I'd no sooner enter the pew than *bingo,* my mind leapt to sex. I was the Sisyphus of lewd thoughts. Would I ever reach that higher plane?

Worthy or not, I was set for confirmation at thirteen. On the great day I dressed in my hand-me-down suit from one of Manzie's shorter musician friends. Roughly altered by my mother, the suit was dark, but not exactly conservative; I was the only confirmand in shoulder pads and bell bottoms.

My knees knocked as I stepped through the rail and up to the altar, to the feet of the bishop himself. He was a heavyset white guy as big as Santa, though without the beard. He wore an enormous hat and a satiny red robe with gold trim and green inlay. He radiated splendor and majesty and the most phenomenal gravitas.

I figured that God must look just like him.

It felt bizarre to be touched by the bishop and anointed with his oil, but then I saw my mother beaming and everything seemed right. When I descended to earth, I was a Soldier of the Lord. I was worthy, after all.

That night I said my prayers with my standard close: *Please, God, help my mother and father.* It would be sinful to leave out my dad. It would be worse to wish him dead, no matter how sore the temptation. I had to push those thoughts away, just as I muzzled myself at confession. I could not rat on him, not to the priest, or to Brother Donald, or to God.

His secret was safe with me.

A single room could not long contain the battling Johnsons. When a railroad flat opened up two doors down, in a ramshackle tenement at 958 Gates Avenue, we moved one more time. I would live there till I married.

Our new home was the best we could do for twenty-seven dollars a month. It was on the second of three floors, over a burnt-out space that once housed a sewing factory. Wallpaper hung peeling in shreds. Garbage layered the roof deck and made our living room smell like a sanitation truck.

We'd run into vermin before, but never like this. At 958 Gates, the rodents and roaches ruled. I drew the middle room, with my parents in front through another curtained doorway. On our first night, I woke up to the pitter-patter of tiny feet atop my thin blanket. Bolting upright in the darkness, I heard rustling and squeaking all around me, a nonstop scampering through the house. My floor was alive with a rodeo of mice, a Helsinki Olympics of mice.

"Ma-ma!" I related in lurid detail just what was going on. I could hear my mother, deathly afraid of mice herself, conferring with my father.

And then my father's drowsy voice: "Go back to sleep. We'll take care of it in the morning."

It was the longest night of my life.

The next day my mother and I set about making the place habitable. We scraped the prehistoric wallpaper with spatulas, to ready it for painting. I began clearing the debris out back. By the second week, the roof no longer resembled a landfill, though it took a while longer to get down to the tarpaper.

The mice were our Battle of the Bulge. We closed all visible holes, but still they ran amok. My father bought traps and set them throughout the house: four in the kitchen, two in the bathroom, one each in the living room and bedrooms. That night the rodeo had a new event. I'd start awake with each *snap*—a dispiriting sound, as it was my job to clear the traps come morning. Clean kills, I found, were the exception. Often I'd discover a mouse thrashing in agony long after its fatal mistake. Sometimes I'd find just half a mouse, a riddle I tried not to probe. Every trap was a Crackerjack box from hell; you never knew what hid inside.

It was horrible, but my father refused to do the job and my mother couldn't do it, so I had to cope. I had to open the little death machines over the toilet and flush the remains. After an especially gory night, I might throw a trap, mouse and all, over the roof deck and into an over-grown backyard. But I couldn't do that very often, because my father got mad if he had to buy too many traps.

To make our evenings more eventful, a storefront church moved into the vacant space downstairs. Though Holy Roller congregations speckled Bed-Stuy, I'd never noticed them till now, when the hubbub buzzed our bedrooms half the night. With my father at work, I'd march downstairs and stand outside the church window, screaming at the zealots to shut up and let us sleep. But my pleas were futile. They'd be too ecstatic to notice.

Maybe it was the mouse blood on my hands, or too many tambourines a-banging, but I began to dream of death. I'd start dwelling on it before sleep: Would I be in the dark for eternity? And what did eternity mean? I'd recently seen *Spellbound*, which scared the stuffing out of me, though I loved Gregory Peck's enunciation. Now it oozed into my nightmares. I was teetering on a high ledge, pitching into a black abyss. I was swirling like water down a drain, and I knew I was dying and that I'd be dead for all time—

I'd wake up empty and trembling, in a claustrophobic tizzy: *I'm going to be dead forever, but I won't even know it's forever. Oh my God!*

I guess I'd never bought into heaven as that one-way trip to the Bahamas. Brother Donald was a here-and-now kind of guy, and the Brooklyn nuns weren't terribly helpful. I couldn't get a grip on a happily-ever-afterlife, or happy endings in general. They were too abstract for me; I found it easier to imagine damnation.

After weeks of my abject begging, my father went to the ASPCA and returned with a gray and white cat. Jingle and I were instantly inseparable. If I was in the house, she was with me. She'd pad along at my side, then stop when I stopped to await my next cue. Whoever heard of a cat that heeled? I used to call her My-Cat-Like-a-Dog.

She was a world-class mouser, and after a time the night sounds abated. The traps fell into recession. With Jingle sleeping by me, my dreams were less morbid. But her talent, I fear, was to her detriment. It couldn't have been healthy to stalk those diseased urban rodents. Less than a year after she came to me, I found Jingle in the bathtub, stiff and still.

"It's your cat," my father said. "You've got to get rid of it."

Tearful, nauseated, I did as I was told. I couldn't bear to touch the corpse, so I used a dustpan and wrapped my cat in newspaper and took her out to the trash. It was a Bed-Stuy burial. It was all I could do.

For my father, drinking was mostly a weekend affair, a way to unwind from his drudge work.

For my mother it was something more: her ticket to ride. By the time we moved to Brooklyn, she drank to get through the day. She didn't miss work the morning after, or stash her pints in a hat box or the broom closet. But whenever she cooked at the stove, there was a water glass filled with ice and several fingers of brown liquid.

Despite her low tolerance for alcohol, my mother drank fast to get *there* fast and stay as long as she could. After two hasty shots, she'd recover her boisterous good humor. After three or four, her speech began to slur, her balance to suffer. She turned truculent and defensive: a cartoon drunk. My father hated seeing her that way, especially around his in-laws. We weren't riffraff, after all. Jackie Johnson might be a wife-beater and a child-abuser, but he was touchy about his dignity, and by extension his bride's.

We saw my mother's family most Saturdays for dinner. They rarely came to Brooklyn, as no one sought a rerun of the night Mom got so crocked that she nearly fell into her stew pot and had to be poured into bed. Besides, Uncle Syl and Aunt Marian had a DuMont television, a bulky wooden box with a square cut out for the screen, and everybody liked to watch the wrestling on Saturday night.

By the time we got to Harlem, my mother was primed for a tall one and the party was on. Aunt Marian favored Rico Rum and Cokes, and drank liberally but under control. Mama Tutt preferred Old Grand-Dad, which she handled as well as your average longshoreman. My mother liked all of the above, in addition to rye or gin, and set sail for the land of the comatose.

Often we were joined by Mr. Elliot Austin, Mama Tutt's companion. A Pullman porter like Uncle Syl, Mr. Austin was a grandfatherly man who'd squeeze me tight and rub his knuckles across the top of my head. I liked him tremendously, even when he'd tease that I was the only one in the family with mattress ticking for hair.

At some point in the evening, without fail, Mr. Austin would extract a sheet of paper from his wallet and ask me to read it. Playing along, I recited my vow from years before: "I will never leave my mother and father, and I want to be a cowboy when I grow up."

Mr. Austin would ask me, "Remember when you wrote that?" I'd smile, abashed at my childishness. And he'd say, "Now don't you be riding off somewhere. I want you to stick around for a while, cowboy."

(The sweet man would be murdered in 1964, stabbed to death on the street for his brown paper bag. It contained Mr. Austin's lunch.)

My grandmother and aunt made roast beef and collard greens and the finest potato salad on the planet. As soon as dinner was ready, my father became Ralph Kramden. Though he couldn't wrest the head of the table from Uncle Syl, he made sure to sit at "the other head." He was always served first, with the largest portions. My mother catered him a special salad, the tomatoes sliced rather than chopped.

To keep the peace, the women waited on His Lordship

with the occasional roll of an eye. As Mama Tutt brought out her transcendent bread pudding, my father placed his coffee order. My mother trotted off to fix it—evaporated milk, two sugars—without a word. She was hostage to my father's nuclear threat, his first-strike detonation. If she did everything right, she might forestall it. She might get through dinner without a scene.

After the table was cleared, Aunt Marian went to the phonograph. If my mother wasn't too tipsy, or my father too grumpy, they might reprise their courtship at the Renaissance Ballroom. It was sublime to see them lindy or foxtrot through the living room, gliding together as one. I'd grin when my mother nestled into her beau's shoulder and winked at me. They could be so graceful, so in love.

After my mother drank a little more, she'd ask her sister to put on Morgana King, the white soul queen. She'd sway in place, her eyes half-shut, and maybe she'd cry a little bit. Her favorite number was "My Funny Valentine," to which she'd sing along:

But don't change a hair for me
Not if you care for me
Stay little valentine staayyy . . .

When it came to melancholy, Morgana King had nothing on Irene Johnson. When my mother sang that ballad, you could see deep down inside her. You could feel the plight of a woman who'd asked for little in life and had gotten considerably less.

Did my father feel undressed by the window my mother opened? Did he taste her sadness? In any case, he was scoffing by the second verse: "There she goes again. That Irene is the only woman I know who can walk in on the *middle* of a picture and cry."

My mother rubbed at her glistening eyes and said, "Shut up, Jackie, shut *up!*" The music went up-tempo and she rallied. I tried to stop her, because I knew what was coming—*No, Mama, not the Shuffle off to Buffalo!*

My mother stomped out the beat till the floor shook. Everyone laughed but my father, who glowered from a couch in the corner, with an ash on his cigarette to defy Isaac Newton. (He held it indefinitely, up to the moment he was offered an ashtray, when it dropped perversely to the rug.)

My mother ultimately shuffled off onto the floor, in a heap. In a family of drinkers, she'd be the first to get pie-eyed and ossified. By the law of the pack, everyone turned on her.

Aunt Marian (a number of sheets to the wind herself): *Fatty, you know you shouldn't drink so much.*

Mama Tutt (several more sheets): *Irene, you can't hold your liquor—just look at you!*

My father (with a grandiloquent shake of his head): *Oh, Irene, can't you slow down? There you go, drunk already! Mm-*mm. *Look at your mother, boy, she drunk already!*

Unrepentant, my mother would snap, "Ah, I don' give a damn!" If I was in range, she might grab me for a sloppy kiss. But this coarse, blowsy woman repelled me, and I let her know it: *Stop it, Mama, you can't even talk!* Her child was the one critic who shamed her, and she'd lash back, "Oh, shut up, you're jus' like your father!"

My grandmother kept the pot stirring. A gifted provocateur, she shuttled between my parents to play the little devil on their shoulders. To my father: *She's out of control. Why can't you do something?* To my mother: *Look at the way he treats you. I don't know why you stay with him.*

Uncle Syl fled Mama Tutt's browbeating for his bedroom and a Mozart string quartet. But my father loved a donnybrook, and my mother felt compelled to defend him. My aunt threw in her two cents, or maybe half a dollar. By the time they sat down for a game of bid whist, they were bickering in quadraphonic sound.

The liquor kept flowing. Mama Tutt disliked my father when she was sober and despised him when soused. Her muttering got louder: *no good . . . lazy . . . evil . . .*

My father knew that his in-laws counted him a slacker. My uncle, a quiet paragon of self-improvement, only made him look the worse. Cast in his old role as pariah, he threw down his cards, cursed people out, and challenged poor Sylvester Mosely to a fight.

Aunt Marian: *Here he goes again.*

Mama Tutt: *All you want to do is cause trouble.*

And my mother: *Jackie, sit down. Don't start this now!*

My father would not sit down. He played his trump, instead. He ruined the party by removing his two prized possessions, my mother and myself. He might never be loved as we were, but he could take his chattel with him and bruise it up to make his point. As my aunt liked to say, "He wants to take the sun out of the sky."

Everyone knew that bad things were brewing back in Brooklyn. But no one would call out my father. He was a chilling figure when crazed.

The older I got, the more stressful our get-togethers. I could chart each evening's course down to its grim unraveling at Gates Avenue. When my father was unhappy, everybody paid, but my mother paid dearest.

I couldn't hit him back for her; I still wasn't big enough. But I found another way to hurt him. I withdrew my love and let him know it; I'd be John E. Johnson Jr. in name only. I would listen to the women's whispered urgings, a mantra echoed by my mother when her man was out of earshot:

Don't you be like him . . .

My birthdays were invariably disappointments. They fell in June, when a boy's fancy turns to Schwinns, but my father never bought me a bicycle and I knew better than to ask. "If we get a bike out here," he'd say, "somebody'll steal it."

It was harder to accept my want of roller skates. When I met my friends at the rink, I'd be the only one in line at the rental counter. With my narrow feet and the loose house skates, it was like wallowing around in bedroom slippers.

I'd remind myself of how poor we were. Wasn't my dad always beefing about his pay and the cost of living? In reality, however, we weren't *that* poor. By the time I reached ninth grade, my last year at Halsey, my father had a permanent job at the post office. My mother worked full-time at the pocketbook counter at Abraham & Straus, the big department store in downtown Brooklyn. Together they must have made more money than most of our neighbors.

But my father was a withholding man, and my mother deferred to him. Their gifts to me were small, though gratefully received. I remember a few records to add to my Ravel: Gershwin's *Rhapsody in Blue,* Rimsky-Korsakov's *Scheherazade,* a Rachmaninoff concerto. (When I spun them on Uncle Syl's hand-me-down phonograph, I'd press a toy stethoscope to the speaker: stereo sound!)

One Christmas I got a cheap guitar. For a time I was obsessed, noodling over the strings for hours. I really wanted to make music. But without any lessons, I gradually lost interest.

The best present was one my father really got for himself: an 8-millimeter projector. When we put on a rented fight film, his old stories came to life. We saw Jack Dempsey robbed by the famous "long count" against Gene Tunney. We cheered when Joe Louis got up off the mat to beat Tony "Two Ton" Galento. We even scanned a grainy souvenir, from 1910, of Jack Johnson's demolition of Jim Jeffries, the Great White Hope.

Boxing was our shared passion, a tacit channel for the baring of our love. Secluded in the sitting room off our kitchen, we'd lean from the couch toward the postcard-sized picture, our shoulders touching, thick as thieves. The films were silent, which was just as well, because my dad supplied his own color commentary. *Look at that, Johnny! He's leaning over and throwing at an angle, you see?* Often he'd back up the projector to show me something I might have missed; I gleefully watched Joe Louis wreck Max Schmeling, Hitler's champion, at least two dozen times. When my father got excited, he'd enlist me for a live-action replay: *Put up your hands, move, move, that's the way, keep your head down, now throw that hook!*

In the fall of 1951, we bought our first television, just in time to see Bobby Thomson torpedo the Dodgers for the National League pennant. (On my knees in prayer as the ball cleared the fence, I collapsed to the floor, while my father hopped up and down in anguish.) Boxing was a regular feature on early TV, and my dad and I had a standing date for the Friday night fights, brought to us by Gillette.

My father was a classicist. To pass his muster, a fighter had to be able to throw a punch and take one, too. He liked the guys with technique *and* toughness: Willie Pep, Sandy Saddler, Ezzard Charles. And Archie Moore, "the Old Mongoose," who was about to snatch the light heavyweight crown at age thirty-nine and hold it for another ten years.

As in everything else, we had our differences, most pointedly over Floyd Patterson, the pride of Bed-Stuy. Floyd had won the Golden Gloves two years running on his way to an Olympic gold medal, and every boy in the neighborhood held him in awe. I remember spotting him once at the Bushwick Theater, with his outlandish pompadour and star's aura. *He doesn't look that big to me,* I whispered to my friends, but behind my bravado I was swooning.

My father was not so enamored. He questioned Floyd's peek-a-boo style and reckoned him vulnerable to a heavy puncher. (Down the road, Sonny Liston would prove my dad right.)

For my father, no fighter could ever match Joe Louis, the champion of the world when we had no one else to root for. For my generation, Louis remained the icon of icons. When I was a little boy back in Washington, boarding a train at Union Station with my parents for New York, I spied a statuesque man in a dress army uniform down the platform. His khaki seemed to be glowing, or maybe it was the light that shines on special people.

"That's Joe Louis!" I pealed, spotting him from the newspapers. When my father walked me over to shake his hand, I was blinded by the light. Louis was doing his bit for special services, fighting exhibitions to boost morale, but I thought he could have pulverized the Luftwaffe and drubbed the Gestapo for dessert.

As much as he adored the Brown Bomber, my father agreed that Sugar Ray Robinson was the best, pound-for-pound, that ever lived. That meant a lot to me, because Sugar Ray was my idol. Though slightly built, he fought with ambidextrous power, seamless grace, and a warrior's heart. Like Jackie Robinson, he inspired me—not so much to become a great athlete, but to be great at *something*.

I patterned my moves after Sugar Ray's when bobbing and weaving with my father. I must have lost something in translation, though, because one day he nailed me with a chopping right. I refused to let him know that he'd buckled me, and made sure it never happened again.

Whenever we went to the Metropolitan, my mother steered us to *Joan of Arc,* by Jules Bastien-Lepage. Joan is standing in her parents' garden, a barefoot peasant girl in a long brown skirt and a drawstring blouse, sleeves up for the next milking. She's depicted at the pivot point of her life, eyes cast heavenward, receiving her revelation and her fate.

At our first run-in, when I was ten or eleven, I said, "Is it a real painting?"

"Yes, it's real," my mother said. "It looks like a photograph, but it really is a painting." As she told me Joan's story, I was riveted and appalled. How could they burn someone so rosy-cheeked, so pure?

As I became a deeper Catholic (and a fevered romantic), Joan moved me more and more. Her innocence, her delicacy as she caressed a single leaf—she was imbued. She was *touched.* The painting was perfect, I thought, save for a trio of hazy saints hovering off to the left. I would have cropped them out, because Joan's face said it all for me.

But my mother loved everything in *Joan of Arc,* including the saints. She had no quarrel with the presence of a few kind spirits.

She was open to any help she could get.

> *I am now 14 years old. Mom Dad fine in new home.*
> —Dictionary entry, December 14, 1952

Another Saturday dinner with Aunt Marian and Mama Tutt. Another time of too much rum and too little tenderness. My father took to yelling as we began our ride home. It was nothing unusual, just his routine invective, but my mother couldn't take it that night. Their feuding escalated on 125th Street. My father's eyes were ablaze, his mouth set in a caustic sneer. As we scaled the ramp to the Triboro Bridge, he jerked back his hand to feign a punch, and my mother flinched.

He did it again, and again, and my mother kept flinching, until she was sobbing despondently. We were past the toll booth and nearly onto the bridge itself—in dense traffic, at forty miles per hour—when she threw open her door and made to hurl herself out.

"Mama, no!" I lunged forward to catch her. My father had no place to pull over; I had to hold fast or she'd be gone. There was a roar of wind and tires and the blare of a horn, too close. The pavement skimmed beneath her, black and deadly.

"Let me go!" she said. My mother was not a small woman, and she sincerely meant to capitulate. But I would not give her up. With the strength people find in extremis, I held her back and closed the door. I kept holding as she cried herself out. I wanted never to let her go.

My father kept his mouth shut into Brooklyn; he knew that he'd gone too far. For several days he seemed strangely withdrawn, not quite in the present, like a man reprieved as the switch was to be thrown. He was shocked by our near calamity, and by knowing it might happen again.

As for me, I made sure to lock the doors when my mother was in the car. I did what I could to make her happy, or at least forgetful that she wasn't. I had to save her—from her husband, from herself, from a life she could neither face nor change.

CHAPTER SEVEN

OUT OF THE GRAB BAG OF HEREDITY, MY HANDS TOOK FROM BOTH sides. I had my father's long fingers and my mother's vascularity, her skein of blood vessels and tendons just under the skin. That was what lured me to Rodin, in the room of his sculptural fragments at the Met: the hands that seemed modeled after mine.

No totems of tranquillity, Rodin's hands. They were dramatic, kinetic, physically stressed. My favorite was a half-clenched bronze. Rising primordial out of its raw material, fingers reared like horses' heads, the work struck me with a force beyond any painting's. It was as though a whole body, a life history, had been compressed from wrist to thumbnail.

At age twelve, I was seized by a need to mold things. My mother bought some self-hardening clay, and soon our windowsills and dressers were crammed with horses and jungle cats. As much as I loved to paint, my aptitude was keener in three dimensions. My hands had their own innate intelligence. Sculpture felt right for me.

By ninth grade, my last year at Halsey, I'd set my sights on Industrial Art, the one public high school to provide it. The test and portfolio were no problems. Breaking the news to Dad was something else. How could I say that I wanted to be a sculptor, a commercial dead end since the nineteenth century? It would be inconceivable to him, a childish pipe dream.

My quandary came to a head one day when he asked about my plans for the future: "You have to have something to make money, you know." My dalliance with the priesthood had faded. What now?

I hemmed and hawed before it came to me, out of some article I'd read: "I want to be a ceramics engineer!" Ceramics was the surface of the future, I explained, and Industrial Art offered a major in it. In truth, I had no more interest in engineering than in animal husbandry, but I knew it was something my father could accept.

Aside from its curriculum, the best thing about the school was its East Side Manhattan address. In Harlem, with Uncle Manzie, I'd sampled *la vie de bohème*. Through my classmates at Halsey, I'd tasted middle-class comforts. I wanted more.

I wanted out.

It took three subway trains to reach my new school. On the third, the uptown Lexington Avenue line, black passengers were few and far between. The cops harassed me as a matter of course, and once frisked me along with a schoolmate. As our fellow riders stared at us with distaste, one of the cops said, "Got a report of some niggers with knives." My friend and I were neatly dressed and loaded with textbooks. Weighing 250 pounds between us, we weren't exactly FBI poster boys. But we knew better than to resist.

I spent three invaluable years at Industrial Art. The Met was blocks away, and I went almost daily on my student pass. I spent hours with friends in the sculpture garden at the Museum of Modern Art. I read Camus and Sartre, and Simone de Beauvoir.

And I met Shelby Gomprecht, my history teacher through high school. Miss Gomprecht was a sparkling young woman with outspoken views. An early advocate of civil rights, a feminist before her time, she swam against the McCarthyite tide. She proposed that slavery spelled the downfall of ancient Greece, and that racial discrimination could do the same to America. "A healthy society," she liked to say, "needs the greatest amount of freedom for everybody." From our first hour together I felt a strong connection, the natural alliance of unconventional minds.

When I brought my new ideas home, I found that my parents mostly shared them. They might not have studied with Henry Steele Commager, as Miss Gomprecht had, but they knew what they were missing.

Her name was Lorraine, my father said as we drove to her flat on Hancock Street. "She's just a friend of mine, and she's really nice," he went on. "I don't want you to think ill of me, but after a man's been with one woman for twenty years, he needs a friend sometimes."

I thought, *He's taking me to meet his girlfriend.* I suppose it was my father's idea of male bonding. It was doomed, of course, from the start.

Lorraine was a coffee-colored woman with processed reddish hair and sharp features. Slightly younger than my mother, she wore her skirt shorter and her perfume thicker, and she was big enough on top to make guys stop and notice.

After receiving us warmly into her studio apartment, Lorraine settled back on her bed to talk. I liked her straightaway. She was lively and available, the type who put the wives on edge when she entered a room. It was clear to me that Lorraine and my father were having an affair, and I didn't get it. What could this attractive, middle-classy woman see in him?

A few weeks later, Lorraine came over to our place with a "boyfriend," to be discreet. But subtlety wasn't my father's long suit, and he made his feelings obvious. He even fixed Lorraine a drink, something he'd never do for his wife. My mother had to know; I could tell she was hurt.

Maybe I felt angry to be part of my father's sordid lie. Or maybe I was a fifteen-year-old kid with percolating hormones and an all-too-quiet nightlife. I turned on the charm, and Lorraine responded as I knew she would: "What a cute son you have!" As we gabbed and laughed together, with meaningful touches of arms and shoulders, my father got that look on his face. But he was cornered. He couldn't object without exposing himself, and he couldn't compete in the glib department because he didn't have it in him.

It must have been quite the comeuppance. In his perverse fashion my father had reached out to me, and I'd slapped his hand away and made him look the fool. I'd hinted that the days of his dominion might be numbered.

His little boy was growing up.

Having a little trouble in French but mom and I are studying and I'm doing better. Mom and dad young as ever and are still the best parents in the world...
        —Dictionary entry, December 20, 1953

My tenth-grade French teacher was a bigot, bad news for the nonwhite kid in her class. At our conference early in the term, she glanced at my quiz scores and told my mother, "I don't see any way that John will be able to pass the Regents exam in the spring."

Failing a major subject would be disastrous, a permanent blot on my transcript. My mother wasn't about to let some "old prejudiced person" destroy my opportunity for college. Though she didn't know French from pig Latin, she guaranteed that I would pass. She drilled me tirelessly on vocabulary and grammar, teaching herself as she went along. It felt like the old days, when she'd taught me to read.

I ultimately earned an 80 on a tough Regents final, one of the higher marks in the class. But my teacher reserved the last word: "John passed the Regents! Let's all give him a round of applause."

At home, our Saturday labor camps remained in force. In the space of half a dozen hours, my mother worked to bring order to her life, or at least to our apartment. She became a changed personality, purse-lipped and pitiless; this was martial law, and she was the marshal. Reveille was 0600 hours. If I slept one minute past, she'd dump my shoes on my shiftless body and bang the side of my bed. We had to move like white rabbits to be first in line at Bohack's, the big grocery store on Broadway. Why? To be back in time to dust and mop and scrub.

Though I hated those Saturday mornings, it never crossed my mind to shirk them. I felt a debt to my parents. I complied without question, except for one wretched dawn when my mother tried to *sweep* me out of bed. I stuck out my hand by reflex, grabbed her broom, and hopped onto the floor with it. Though I was acting in self-defense, she cowered back. For the first time I was conscious of being taller than she was.

"Just like your father," she said, which seemed to me uncalled for.

I must have been cursed that morning. Upon arriving at Bohack's, I went to the cashier with my bagful of soda bottles, to be redeemed for two cents apiece. Normally I inspected them for roaches and water bugs beforehand, but we'd been running late that day. As I unloaded my booty onto the counter, a cavalcade of crawlers skittered out, like a science fiction movie after the atomic test.

The cashier, a middle-aged white woman, was not pleased. "Ahhhh, *roaches!*" she shrilled. "Get those dirty bottles *out* of here!" Her customers glared at me in revulsion; now I knew how Gregor Samsa felt. My mother, close by in the baked goods section, pretended not to know me, though I could see her stifling a laugh. (*Et tu, mama?*) I put my tainted goods back into the bag and slunk outside, penniless and disgraced.

The track coach entered me at middle distances, to mediocre results. I did my best running at a sprint, in competition with my father. For years I'd been racing him, occasionally barefoot on the beach, more often down our block to the corner of Ralph, a stretch of sixty or seventy yards. I wore my Keds, my dad his rubber-soled work shoes, and for years I'd been finishing second. My father would keep it close for a while to tease me before pulling away. He was long and powerful, super fast. I wanted more than anything to beat him, to show him how good I was.

There is a stage in every process where small, incremental advances—barely noticed for months or even years—suddenly build to a critical point, and everything changes. For my father and me, the point came on a spring day a month or two shy of my sixteenth birthday. We lined up on the sidewalk in front of our house, and for twenty yards raced side by side, as usual. He put on his little burst and chortled, out of habit. But his amusement was short-lived, because *I was still there.* For a stride or two I savored the flummoxed look on his face. Then I turned it on and disappeared. I crushed him.

Puffing as he reached the corner, my father said, "Damn, you can run." Then he said, "I bet you can't do it again." We raced back and I *really* whipped his ass, because now I was more relaxed. He never beat me after that.

The following Halloween, a night of perennial anarchy in Bedford-Stuyvesant, three younger teenaged boys ripped the gate off an iron fence and hurled it atop our used Lincoln, denting the hood. Seeing the mini-terrorists in flight, my father said, "Go get 'em, Johnny"—he sicced me on those boys like a dog. They were startled when I ran them down; I'd caught up in a hurry. I knocked one to the ground and kept the other two busy until the cavalry arrived. My father warned the boys in the holiday spirit: "You come around here again and we'll beat the shit out of you!"

Against the outside world, my father and I stood united. Once we stopped at a gas station near the Williamsburg Bridge, and a burly customer started giving my dad a hard time. The guy looked like he might be about to hit someone. I jumped out of the car and went at him, ready to get it on.

My father was shocked by how difficult it was to restrain me, by the white heat of my anger. He saw another side of me that day.

As I came of age, I felt more protective toward my parents. Each day after school, I met my mother at Abraham & Straus and caught the train back home with her. I worried when my father went off to his graveyard shift. I knew he'd be passing some bad people on their stoops, and how little it took to set them off.

I would do anything to spare my dad from harm. I wonder if he knew how much I loved him, in my way.

Brenda Hunter was one of the few black students in an academic track at Industrial Art. She was shy and birdlike, terribly sweet, and in my junior year she became my steady girlfriend. After school we'd stroll around town and I'd carry her books. On nice days we'd go up to the

Bronx Zoo. Her mother, a Pentecostal who worked as a domestic, thought I was perfect.

Brenda lived on 125th Street, in the heart of Harlem. When walking her home I'd tangle with the local talent, lazy boys who saw an easy mark. Twice I was threatened with a knife. But I didn't scare and I knew how to fight. After word leaked out that I was one of those crazy Negroes from Gates Avenue, people let me be.

Though Brenda and I often were alone in her apartment, we stayed on our best behavior. I was a good Catholic, still going to confession, and my girlfriend chaster than chaste. We were the urban version of *Ozzie and Harriet* until one Saturday afternoon, when we became amorous in Brenda's apartment.

Standing just inside her bedroom door, Brenda said, "Did you touch my breast?" I denied it, but I was lying. I had never touched anything so marvelous in my life, albeit through a bra, a shirt, and a heavy sweater. We kissed and hugged. I tugged on Brenda's shirt to forge an interior route to the summit. I was nearly there when the avalanche crashed on my head.

"Brenda, Brenda, omigod, what are you *doing*, Brenda?" Returning from a movie with my mother, of all people, Mrs. Hunter had a clear line of sight into her daughter's bedroom. We were breathless and panicked; Brenda's shirt was out and her glasses askew. She stood there with her big eyes, looking guilty and so very innocent. Mrs. Hunter breathed one final *Oh, Brenda, no!* before losing her balance and toppling onto the living room sofa.

I rushed out with a red-faced defense: "Mrs. Hunter, so help me God, I-I didn't do anything! Nothing's happened, I swear to God!"

Shaking her head, my mother said, "Okay, John, time for us to go now." She didn't seem too upset—at least by comparison to Mrs. Hunter, who was splayed on the couch hyperventilating.

On the train my mother looked at me fondly and said, "You have to be smarter than that, Johnny." I sat speechless with shame and the unfairness of it all. Here I was, in my second year of high school. Everyone I knew back in Brooklyn had been screwing for years; they probably had grandchildren by now. Little Johnny Boy, meanwhile, felt one tiny breast (Brenda was very slight, nearly concave) and people went into convulsions. *If this is what sex is like,* I thought miserably, *I'll never have another erection.*

Mrs. Hunter had no grounds for worry. In 1955, good boys and nice girls didn't go all the way before marriage. Brenda stayed my steady till college, and I left her a virgin, just like me.

I had two left feet at school dances; I couldn't step to "Cherry Pink" to save my life. But I acquitted myself nicely in the cha-cha or the mambo with the family in Harlem. I was my mother's favorite partner, and Aunt Marian's as well, whether the music played fast or slow.

When the song ended and we slid to a halt, my aunt would crane up at me and say breathlessly, "Oh, Johnny Boy, you're just the *handsomest!*" Or the smartest, or the nicest, and so forth. I was quite the guy in my family. True, the competition wasn't stiff. Uncle Syl would either be out of town or holed up with his books, and my father was my father. Flattery had no spot to land save on me.

There was the faintest tinge to our affinity, something that made me the least bit uneasy as I'd shift to an Ellington ballad with my mother or aunt. It wasn't so large as a molecule, or even an atom—more a sexual neutrino, lacking charge or mass. Never acknowledged, much less acted upon, it had no existence of its own. But it was there.

Like Stanley Kowalski and other legendary brutes, my father was hypersensitive to slights. When the women bubbled, "Johnny, you are really something," the comparison hung in the air: that my father was nothing. I felt him stewing in the corner like a spurned suitor. Like the ex-boyfriend with the acid in his cup, the razor blade tricked between his fingers.

The more attention I drew, the worse the backlash for my mother in Brooklyn. Back home my father would be thin-skinned and thick-headed, a free-swinging tyrant over all that he surveyed. Back home he would remind the little woman, none too gently, that he was the man in her life.

Her one and only.

Till death do them part.

If sculpting takes you into a three-dimensional world, it was an apt venture for me in high school. During the week I apprenticed downtown with Nat Choate, who'd worked on the friezes at Rockefeller Center and taught me to cast huge pieces in the old tradition. On weekends, a conscript in the Beat Generation, I made a beeline to the Village. Arm in arm with my artsy friends, my black beret in place, I'd take in a Bergman film or sip espresso at a coffeehouse where Allen Ginsberg or my hero James Baldwin might be reading.

To augment my summer pay as a stock clerk in Macy's men's sock department, I sketched portraits on the street. I felt headily independent. I remember buying a pair of gorgeous wool pants—midnight blue, sleek enough for flamenco—and bristling when my father questioned the price. "I'm making money," I reminded him. He was confounded, nonetheless. How could I spend so much on a vanity?

The divide between my home and where I *lived* kept widening. I'd get off the train at Gates Avenue in my

British duffel coat and desert boots, or my Joe College ensemble (white bucks, letterman jacket), and fall into a stream of bellbottoms and brimmed hats. The transition jarred me every time, and fashions were the least of it. After seven years in Bed-Stuy, I still felt like a transient. I'd skirted the community's Boy Scouts and basketball teams, and hanging out, as we've seen, was never an option.

I hated the poverty around us, the way it ground people up with their hopes for something better. I remember walking home from the Bushwick Theater after seeing *Rififi*, the chic French caper film. Back on the bleak streets, I had to stop and lean against a car. I was woozy. The local atmosphere no longer sustained me.

I spent less and less time at home. I still rose to my Saturday duty, but without my old military snap. "All you do is eat and sleep here," my mother complained. She was losing her hold.

As teacher and student, our roles reversed. When I took my mother to the Museum of Modern Art, a second home for me by then, I showed off my new knowledge— the difference between Impressionism and Cubism, the whimsy of Marcel Duchamp. My mother made appreciative noises (*Oh that's nice, I like that, gee that's pretty*), but she wasn't one to stop and digest things. As my father's wife, she pulled to the beat of a crazed coxswain. She was used to living in a hurry.

I wanted to take her deeper. When we reached *Hide and Seek,* Tchelitchev's sensuous tree of life, I said, "Wait a minute, Mom. Let's look at this in a different way, not just as a picture of a tree. You have to *look* to see it."

She took a step back and studied for a minute, and then she said, "Oh, my goodness." Plunging down the rabbit hole, she solved the puzzle of baby heads within the liquid flora. She was excited and a little bit scared, for what sort of hide-and-seek was this? (It was a seeking in-

side your soul, and there are creepy things down there.)
But the longer my mother paused, the more she liked
that painting, and she'd refer to it often in years to come.
A willing study, she came to admire Van Gogh and Gau-
guin, Picasso and Braque and Modigliani. She entered a
new sphere.

I know that my mother treasured that afternoon with
me. But it had to be bittersweet for her, too, because she
saw firsthand that I was going places she could not follow.

All my life, she and my father had demanded that I
excel. They pushed me to be better and more disciplined, to stay ahead of the pack. In my senior year in
high school, I drove myself like a crazy person. I became
captain of the track team, head of the National Honor Society, student body president. In a predominantly white
school, I was voted most likely to succeed.

Everyone knew I was going places. What my parents
hadn't banked on was that I'd be moving away from
them—and not merely from their zip code, a given, but
from their frame of reference. While I had no wish to
abandon them, I'd distanced myself nonetheless, like
some lonely immigrant child packed off to the golden
shores.

I was leaving them behind.

At seventeen I was nearly six feet tall, lean and wiry
from track and tough as a matter of principle. My father
took note. When we sparred at a picnic, we were evenly
matched. After a preface of flashy footwork, my dad
would hulk in on me to push me off balance. I'd dance
around and snicker at the backhanded compliment. John
Sr. was past forty. I could have picked my round to deck
him, though it never occurred to me to try.

I was watching TV in the living room one evening
when he stomped past me to the kitchen doorway. I

could tell by the jut of his neck that he was steamed at my mother. I heard him go *up;* he was going to slap her. He was going to hurt her, again, and I had to stop him.

I stood and opened my mouth . . . for an empty breath. I was still afraid of him, you see. I feared his temper and his mouth, his anger with no bottom. He was my father. No matter how big or strong I got, he would hold the upper hand.

In my moment of immobility, he swung. My mother cried out in pain and disarray. I'd witnessed this a hundred times before; I was *seeing* it for the first time. I came unstuck, like a sluggish transmission shifting into gear. I found the words from the last time I'd stood up to him, as a skinny eight-year-old on a Harlem stairway.

Don't you hit my mother!

I changed registers mid-injunction, from a choked falsetto to a gruff baritone, from a frightened kid to a bona fide adversary. My silence was broken. The gauntlet was thrown.

My father wheeled to confront me: "What did you say?" He was enraged, and astonished.

"Don't you hit my mother!" My voice was steadier this time.

My father took three quick steps toward me and I thought, *Oh Lord, now I've done it.* My adrenaline ran riot. I hated the bastard; I burned to do him in. Nostrils flared, I put up my dukes: another surprise. He swung with his left, but it reached me in a weird anticlimax, in a weak-ass jab that I ducked with ease.

Before my father could reload or I could think about countering, my mother went berserk. Dressed in her nightgown, screaming incoherently, she threw open our door and started pell-mell down the stairway.

What was she going to do, run down the street half-naked? Hurl herself in front of a car? The battle aborted, I dashed down the stairs and—using the banister as a long horse—vaulted over my mother to the landing. I spun around and checked her, which took some doing, while my father looked down at us and said, "Irene, you get yourself up these stairs!" I literally dragged her back into the apartment.

It would take me a while to decipher my mother's behavior, to see that she'd contrived the diversion, her dignity be damned. She had more common sense than the combatants. She knew a fistfight would leave lasting scar tissue, no matter who came out on top.

I would submit, however, that her drama was unnecessary. True, I'd stood prepared to defend us. But after slipping my dad's halfhearted swing, I was already turning away when my mother made her dash. I didn't want to hurt my father. Had I given in to my anger, I'd be regretting it to this day.

Something changed after our showdown at the testosterone corral. My father was leery of me. I'd beveled off some of his manic rage; he still railed and ranted, to be sure, but without so much foaming at the mouth. He was a modulated monster.

He never hit me again, nor my mother in my sight.

I grew up in a pro-Roosevelt household. My parents were crazy about Franklin and Eleanor because they were "for the people." When I was seven years old, my father took me out on a cold day in Washington to stand on the street and watch FDR's casket roll by.

I never lost my affection for Eleanor, the embodiment of my liberal ideals. What other rich white ladies were visiting Africa or drumming up support for the United Nations? When we needed a speaker at school for a special assembly, Miss Gomprecht and I decided to write her to see if she were free.

The principal seemed skeptical: "Don't you think you ought to invite someone a little more realistic?" Our letter wasn't all that eloquent, but for some reason Mrs. Roosevelt accepted. Everybody was stunned. Come the great day, before the assembly where I'd introduce our guest, the principal called me to his office to meet her.

I shook my idol's hand on a cloud. While I cannot recall a word she said, I remember her regal height (abetted by an extravagant hat), and her kind, homely face. I remember her patrician voice as she spoke to me as though I mattered. That day I felt touched by greatness, indeed ready to take on the world.

—*To John Johnson, a wonderful student of history and government because he is a wonderful human being. I wish to pass on to you the work of my teacher, because you feel for your fellow man just as I do. But you have more courage and will do more . . .*
—Inscription by Miss Shelby Gomprecht in a gift copy of *Living Ideas in America,* edited by Henry Steele Commager

The day I turned eighteen, shortly after graduation, my father declared, "You've got to learn how to drink." At a bar on Ralph Avenue by the El, he ordered me a rum and Coke and himself a whiskey, and we proceeded to get drunk as skunks.

Talk inevitably turned to my father's favorite subject, the fairer sex. He said, "You've got to be careful with women. They want to rule you, you know." Soon I was bantering with one of the barmaids, which amused him no end: "Hey, she's kind of liking you." We sat and drank as pals, braying at our lame jokes, and by the time we left I could barely talk.

As my childhood formally ended, my father and I reached a détente. Our rapprochement came of wariness and weariness more than a new mutual esteem. If anything, it was the opposite. The less fearsome my father became, the less tied I felt to him. Fear had anchored our relationship. Fear had kept me attentive, as prey attends the predator.

Unafraid, I would be off with the tide, free to drift from my father's domain. To go so far, I thought, with the hubris of youth, that he would never get me back.

CHAPTER EIGHT

It has been 3 years since I last wrote in this book! Now going to CCNY. Having a little trouble. Mom and Dad fine and sweet as ever ...

—Dictionary entry, November 18, 1956

ON MY FIRST DAY AT CITY COLLEGE, I RAN INTO A BAN THE BOMB march and fell right in step. My cohorts were mostly Jewish graduates of elite high schools like Stuyvesant and Brooklyn Tech. Fewer than one percent of CCNY's full-time, day-session students were black, yet I'd never felt more at home. There was an important relationship between black people and Jewish liberals in those days. Our ideas transcended color.

For years my father had declared, "If I have to work five jobs, you're going to go to college. You're going to make something of yourself." When the time came, though, money was scarce. After I'd turned down several out-of-town schools, it was a coup to be admitted to the poor man's Harvard, where my sole expense would be carfare. I'd soon discover, however, that the hardest part of City College was not getting in, but staying in.

"Take a look to your left and to your right," said the dean at our freshman orientation. "Two of the three of you will not be here at graduation."

A few days later, the track coach saw me working out and invited me onto the varsity. In short order I set a school record in the 60-yard dash. My teammates called me "Breeze," which is what they felt when I passed them.

In the Renaissance tradition, I opted to major in history rather than art. I took too many credits, ran afoul of a hostile professor, and by November I was foundering. The dean's warning seemed prophetic.

All my life I'd been geared toward this step. But when I finally pushed through the door (the first Johnson to get past high school, and wasn't Johnny Boy something?), it felt as though my saga was complete. I was tired of striving; I'd burned out at eighteen.

I performed so poorly first semester that they placed me on probation. Worse, I had to bring in a parent to be officially reinstated. I had to listen as the advisor told my father—that dunce of an ignoramus!—that I'd be out unless I straightened up.

They threw me off the track team and referred me to a therapist. I told her, "Listen, I just want to mambo. If you just let me mambo for a little bit, everything will be fine." City College was my first taste of freedom, and I needed my bite of the apple.

That spring I changed my major to art and gathered myself. The alternative—to fail and fall short, to follow in Dad's footsteps—was too gruesome to contemplate.

By 10:00 we were watching the kitchen clock, trading pregnant glances, itching for the breadwinner to get lost. By 10:30 he was out the door to the BMT on Broadway, to catch the first of three trains to the General Post Office in Manhattan and be on the floor, at his box, by midnight on the dot.

We waited a bit longer, in case he'd forgotten his umbrella or house keys. We were eager but cagey. Not until eleven did I leave on my appointed rounds.

Ding dong, the man was gone. Time to make merry!

I hot-walked down Gates Avenue, pushing to a sprint as I passed the deserted Borden's Milk factory. My destination was a low-lit Irish bar at the corner of Gates and Broadway—the Blarney Stone, if memory serves. I pushed open the battered door, into an aromatic fog of cold cuts and beer. They knew me as a regular. I'd been a patron since junior high, when the managers would turn a blind eye to that nice kid from down the block.

There was nothing like the Blarney Stone's corned beef or pastrami sandwiches, with mustard and pickles and red peppers on the side. The counterman shaved the meat by hand and usually threw in a little extra. He fanned the marbled slices on a long roll, to be cut in half: dinner for two.

On the way back I might make a second stop. My mother was a proper woman. She wouldn't leave the house at night without her husband, much less step into a liquor store. It was left to me to do it for her.

I started drinking with my mother the summer after high school. By the middle of my freshman year at City College, we were partying two or three evenings a week. Mom's libations of choice were cheap and sweet: Thunderbird wine and a godawful concoction called Rock 'n' Rye. (A pint bottle of Thunderbird cost $1.20, as noted in its jingle: *It's Thunderbird, once or twice. Okay, Thunderbird, what's the price? Sixty twice.*)

By 11:20, we were unwrapping the sandwich and opening the first bottle. I was old enough to know that my companion had a drinking problem, but I could not say no to her. I sensed the urgency of her need.

My mother lived a rigorously unexamined life. In public she performed in one continual stage moment, striding the boards with a smile slapped in place. But after the curtain fell, and her audience departed, she was in trouble. If she'd slowed down to ruminate about her lot, I believe she might have killed herself. Or grown morose and joyless, a suicide in waltz time.

Her solution was not to slow down. When there was nowhere to run, my mother clicked her heels thrice and kept reality at bay with a bottle.

As I sipped, my mother gulped; she had pain to be deadened, pronto. By her second glass, as we talked and laughed and watched what was left on TV, I felt her sadness receding. For a fleeting hour or two, in the quiet of the night, there was no one to judge or oppress her. She was smashed again. She was safe for another day.

Some might wonder at a mother who imbibed with her still teenaged son. To be fair, she demanded more temperance of me than of herself. Were I to get tipsy at a family affair, she'd be put off: *Wait a minute, is Johnny drunk?* In fact, I was self-governing. I was better at holding my liquor, and Mom showed me the graphic downside of overdoing it. (My parents were role models with a twist.)

No, I cannot blame her. My mother was a sensitive, talented person who lived in torment, and Thunderbird was the best she could do without a prescription.

Toward one in the morning, as we drained the second pint, we'd be openly in league against John Sr. "He's jealous and evil," my mother would say. "Don't you ever be like him."

With my own tongue loosened, I might reply, "Why don't you leave him? I *hate* him."

My mother would turn on a dime: "Don't you say that, you don't mean that." My hatred was part of our conspiracy, our closeness, and she had fueled it with a thousand grins and grimaces behind the ogre's back. But she also knew to keep it from going too far. She worked on the knife's edge with me.

Once I came home late and found her crawling about the living room on all fours, impressively drunk. Her bridgework had dropped out of her mouth and she was too blind to find it. As I tracked down her teeth, revolted, I resolved to stop drinking with her. Our little soirees no longer seemed so harmless.

I kept my resolution for weeks, until I brought a classmate home for a painting party. My father had already left for work—no great loss, as he'd made it clear he wouldn't help. He refused on principle to work around the house, save for breaking whatever he tried to fix.

My mother supplied the paint, the brushes, the music (a radio tuned to rhythm and blues), and liquid refreshments in the 80 proof range. After we finished the living room, my friend Tony and I attacked the kitchen, while my mother moved to the bathroom. Half an hour later, I found her teetering on a chair, swathing the overhead light bulb with gold enamel trim paint. She'd already covered the other bulbs in the house, along with most of our doorknobs. As the knobs were glass and the paint oil-based, I knew that it would not dry.

My mother's face was wildly spattered. In her painter's cap and ragged housedress, she looked like a clown from the Jackson Pollock Circus. I said, "Ma, you've got to stop." I helped her down from the chair and relieved her of her brush, and set about wiping the doorknobs. Tony, meanwhile, climbed barefoot into the tub to deal with the bathroom ceiling, which my mother had overlooked.

It soon became apparent that Tony had partaken of one too many Rock 'n' Ryes. By the time I caught up with him, there was more paint puddling the bathtub than on the ceiling. When I proposed that we adjourn, he gratefully agreed and fell out on the living room couch.

My father came home early that morning, around six o'clock. He went to the bathroom and found his hand smeared with gold paint. (I'd missed a few spots.) He turned on the living room light and beheld a snoring stranger with paint-splashed feet on his couch. He smelled something burning; the golden bulb had begun to smoke. He sounded like Papa Bear after Goldilocks's crime spree.

"What the hell?" he said. "What the *hell?*"

I struggled out of bed to meet him, with my mother weaving behind me and Tony stirring to some facsimile of consciousness. My father looked at us and demanded, "What the hell is going on in this house? Everything is *painted.*"

I could tell that he was in a good mood, and unlikely to go bonkers in front of an outsider. So I copped a plea: "Don't blame me and Tony. Ma painted the light bulbs."

My father said, "Was she drinking?"

Since my mother was shambling about like a zombie on sedatives, and you could smell her breath from ten paces, I saw no point in a cover-up. "Well," I said, "she had a little sip."

My mother began to protest and I steeled myself . . . when we heard a welcome sound. My father was *laughing.* When something really tickled him, he would double over and whoop like a hyena until he gasped for breath.

My mother relaxed. I felt giddily uplifted, as I always did when my father was happy. It was like the sun breaking through after days of stormy weather, and soon we were whooping helplessly with him. Tony fell in love with my parents, and the night of Mom's paint job passed into family lore.

To get home from school on the subway, I transferred from the IND line to the BMT at Delancey Street. I was on the platform one afternoon when I saw an older man peer at the sign overhead, then look down at a scrap of paper. Something about him seemed familiar.

After people squeezed between us, I kept looking for the man till they cleared. I registered his aquiline features and light brown skin. I stepped up to him and said, "I think you're my grandfather. Is your name Tutt?"

For a moment he was tongue-tied; it was he. I had found the needle in the genetic haystack. "Yeah," he said at last, "my name is Tutt."

I said, "Come on, I'll take you to your daughter," and we boarded the train to Gates Avenue.

Tutt had not seen his twin girls since deserting them more than thirty years before, nor had he ever called or written. My mother never spoke of the man; I knew him only from yellowing photographs. But for some reason he'd been moved to look her up and now he was in our apartment, hat in hand, a rumor sprung to life.

I said, "Mom, I have someone here to see you. It's your father." I think she knew it before the words left my mouth. She must have seen herself in that wrinkled face as I had.

For an awkward moment, both sides stood there agape. The daughter was stunned, the father throttled. Finally Tutt reached out, and I could see that he wanted a Hollywood moment of reconciliation. But my mother stiffened in his arms. She gave him a polite pat, then broke free.

They sat at the dining room table and talked for an hour or so. Then Tutt got up and left. I guess it was a hard habit for him to break.

The miracle left no footprint. My grandfather vanished, this time for good.

I was like any other wise-ass college kid, only more so, as my rebellion was overdue. At home I'd sit at the head of the table to get my father's goat. He'd say, "C'mon, now, you got to move." He'd be loud and nasty until I complied.

"This is bullshit," I'd say. "Why don't you let somebody else sit there for a change?"

To punish me, my father would pontificate on one of the myriad topics he knew nothing about. I'd bite my tongue—*Don't get involved, don't do it*—but he was a master puller of strings. One evening he announced, "It's a known fact that men are intellectually superior to women."

"Oh my God," I said. "Where did you get *that* from?"

"Everybody knows it. You don't see any woman scientists or doctors, do you?"

"Wait a minute—what are you talking about? Have you ever heard of Madame Curie? Do you know what she did?"

"I know," he said, "that she didn't go to a medical school in *this* country."

My father never let facts spoil a good argument. He could go on forever, repeating himself like a child. If I challenged him, he'd turn sarcastic: "You don't know everything, Mr. College Boy."

And then defensive: "I'm still your father—*I'm still your father!*"

And then, inevitably, livid. "God *damn* it!" he'd say, knocking his chair back as he jumped up from the table. "I broke my hump for you people, and you don't appreciate what I've done!"

"But Jackie—"

"Shut up, Irene!"

I had to know when to back down. If I failed to defer in time, the debate would swell into a tantrum, the tantrum into a jihad. He'd turn on my mother, gibing that dinner was late or her housekeeping shoddy—charges hard to bear, as my father had yet to wash dish one.

I put up with him because he was dangerous. It was no good to thrust my mother into a free-fire zone, for what might happen when I wasn't there? So I'd tune the bully out. I'd do the dishes and think about the time (coming soon, now) that I'd fly away.

I opened the box and proudly held up its contents: a khaki pea coat, courtesy of the ROTC. I'd joined to avoid being drafted, but mainly for a warm winter coat.

My mother took one look and broke into tears. I assured her that I wasn't heading off to battle, wars being hard to come by in 1957. She stayed inconsolable. The pea coat proclaimed that I now belonged to the world, beyond her help or protection. Little Johnny Boy was all grown up, and there would be no bringing him back.

In the spirit of full disclosure, I had another reason to switch my major, beyond my academic troubles. The art department was brimming with pretty girls.

Interracial romance still turned heads in those days. When I walked with a friend by the Met, drivers would shout out their windows, *Look at the monkey with the white milk!* But none of us cared. By my sophomore year, I'd broken up with Brenda and was dating a coed named Laura Shapiro, whose parents owned a country home upstate. I fit into the middle class easily, if not quite seamlessly. When Laura and a friend asked me on a trip to Provincetown, they struck out. I had yet to go on a vacation; I could not conceive of such a thing.

I came to know superb artists at City College, notably André Girard, a protégé of Georges Roualt. On weekends André would invite me to his home in suburban Rockland County to work on our canvases. He'd painted everything in the house: the tablecloths, the drapes. When I met his wife, a quintessentially charming Frenchwoman, he nodded toward me and said, "He has the dreams he can do this."

I had my first croissant at André's, my first café au lait. I met Jean Casadesus, the concert pianist and André's son-in-law, then in town for a performance. I tagged along with them to a church hall in Nyack, where Jean rehearsed his Debussy and André set up his easel to paint, fired by *Golliwog's Cakewalk*. I lived in a state of enchantment that weekend. (It is no accident that I live in Rockland County today.)

By night I dreamed of Paris. By day I made paintings and sculptures, which I lugged home on the subway. Big pieces were safer than smaller ones at Gates Avenue, where my mother might elbow a figurine when sloshed.

Often I'd spend Sundays painting in my room. With one of my first oils, an expressionist Christ-like figure, I remember feeling that some higher power had guided my brush. I came out and told my mother, "I think I've been touched by the hand of God!" She thought the painting was wonderful, *wonderful*; I thought she was very insightful.

My father, who went to museums about as often as churches, seemed unmoved by my breakthroughs—until he saw my cab driver. I'd painted my subject up-close-and-personal, in the same muddy umber as the background: a life in monotone. When my father happened upon the portrait leaning on my dresser, he stopped and began to cry. "How," he said, "did you know how to paint my dad?"

George Johnson passed away eight years before my birth, and we didn't even own a good picture of him. If anything, I'd had *my* father in mind. The painting was my homage to all the men who worked too hard, who wore their caps screwed on like crowns of thorns, who suffered without tribute.

Did my father grasp my intention? I cannot be sure.

But as he stood transfixed by the small canvas, I think that he beheld his own purgatory. He was genuinely moved. We had a moment of connection, triangulated through an ancestor I'd never met.

By then my father had been promoted to a customer service window on the day shift. During Christmas rush he manned a small substation on the street corner, a booth molded in the shape of a mailbox. When I went to see him and say hello, I met a few of his co-workers. "Ah, you're the painter," one said. "You want to draw me?"

Another man said, "Well, your father sure does like you. Your father sure is proud of you."

I blushed to hear of my dad's boasting. His pride was a driving force in me, valued all the more for how rarely it surfaced.

> *I have started a new page in this dictionary as I have started a new page in my life and probably the most important. For the first time I found the one person I shall love forever through time and space. Adrienne has become my life. . . . Mom & Dad are more than ever the best parents in the world.*
> —Dictionary entry, September 26, 1958

During the summer following sophomore year, after lying about my age to land a job designing window displays, my heart flew to another girl in our crowd. Adrienne had grown up in a corner apartment overlooking the Bronx Zoo. She was a stellar painter and a gifted student who'd burst into City College at sixteen. She had an Audrey Hepburn ponytail that I found irresistible, and she could really, really dance.

I often brought her out to Gates Avenue for dinner, along with other college friends. They were wild about my mother, who'd hug them and cook up a storm and say, "Anyone my Johnny brings home, I love."

I was keen to show off my parents, except when my father played the petty tyrant. If an ashtray sat five feet from his chair, and my mother was entertaining on the roof deck, he thought nothing of calling out, "Irene, would you get this ashtray for me?" It drove me crazy when my mother fetched for him, and I could feel our guests frowning. We'd start running for the damn ashtray ourselves—*No, no, don't worry, I'll get it!* ("You'll have to forgive him," I'd tell my friends later. "He's a jerk.")

At dinner it got tense when talk turned to politics. If my father wasn't on the wrong side, he was on the right side for the wrong reasons, and we'd go at it hammer and tongs. One night he said, "You think you know so much?"

Seeing me redden, my mother said, "Jackie, leave him alone."

"No, Irene, he thinks he knows everything." He turned back to me for the crusher: "You think you're better than me?"

My father had my number. I *did* think I was better than him, and smarter and nicer and better-looking. I exulted in showing him up, especially after a drink or two. The prettier the girl I'd imported, the worse my father would behave, and the harder I'd strive to outdo him. We had a cutthroat competition where none should have existed.

Once or twice I caught him looking at Laura or Adrienne in an unsettling way, but I let it pass. No harm done, I thought, and lord knows we didn't need another reason to fight.

Adrienne's parents had immigrated from Belgium, where they'd lost relatives to the Holocaust. At one point they owned the largest fur outlet in New York City, but the family fortunes plummeted when Adrienne was in high school and her father died. For her mother, an emphatic woman half my size, my trespass was the ultimate insult. "I'll never accept this," she said, after hearing me profess my love. "Never, never, never!"

We eloped in the spring of my senior year, marrying in a Harlem housing project, shortly after learning that Adrienne was pregnant. Our justice of the peace had a dickens of a time with the bride's name: "And do you, *Adrieneneh*—" I corrected him twice, then gave up. He had no trouble with "John."

We parted for our respective homes that night and broke the news the next morning. Though Adrienne's mother had softened by then, some relatives sat shiva.

My mother mourned more subtly. While she loved Adrienne, she fretted that we were too young to be parents and that my schooling would be disrupted. (To support my budding family, I'd taken an advertising job at W. T. Grant and switched my classes to night session.) I knew, too, that she felt a wrenching loss. Now she would be alone in the house with *him*.

For me, moving out was a godsend, and a timely one at that. Aunt Marian and Uncle Syl were relocating with Mama Tutt to a larger apartment three blocks north. (Shortly thereafter, Uncle Syl would flee to a new life, and ultimately a new wife, in Florida.) Their old flat on 148th Street was perfect for the newlyweds: eighty dollars a month for an ample space within walking distance of City College. There was even an extra room for a studio.

With no time or money for a honeymoon, we set up housekeeping on the spot. My commercial art was dull work, yet I felt emancipated, nearly weightless. I was free of Bedford-Stuyvesant, beyond its gravitational field. Who knew where I was headed? Enough to know it would be someplace new; enough to know it would devour my past.

Little Adrienne is a wonderful wife and a beautiful pregnant mommy. I love my dearest Adrienne. . . . [Mom and Dad] are fine and youthful as ever. Perhaps I love them more than I have ever in my life since I [no longer] live at 958 Gates, because one truly realizes the value of something when he doesn't have it all the time.

— Dictionary entry, July 2, 1960

We took a Lamaze class, very avant-garde. My expertise went for naught, however, as the doctor sent me into exile midway through Adrienne's twenty-hour labor. A potential complication, he said.

I sat in the waiting room at Columbia Presbyterian, worried to distraction. I had fancied having a girl, a miniature of her mom, but that didn't seem important anymore. I just wanted a healthy baby.

Then I heard the magic words: "It's a boy, and they're both fine."

When I laid eyes on my firstborn son, in his bassinet behind the glass, he looked like a little pink amphibian— but the cutest, cleverest amphibian in the nursery. A current of joy coursed through me, from my scalp to the soles of my feet. I had never felt so much a man.

How different life would be for my child! He would grow in a gentle home, never spanked or slapped or frightened to tears. When my father learned we were pregnant, he asked if we'd name a boy John, to sustain the line. And I said, "The last thing I'm going to do is name him John." We called him Eric instead, *Eric Justin Johnson,* just right for the corner of a canvas or a novel's title page.

On that day of his birth, I swore my son a solemn oath: *You're going to have the best childhood in the world, my Eric. And I'm going to be the best father. I'll always be there for you.*

I had no idea how tough a promise it would be to keep.

With Adrienne sleeping, I rode out to Gates Avenue to celebrate. My mother was crying and smiling and pumping me for details for Aunt Marian and Mama Tutt, who hung on the phone. My father kept repeating, "Can you believe this? Can you *believe* this?"

We sat at the kitchen table and toasted the new arrival. We recounted old stories and laughed our heads off, and toasted some more. I got drunk, which my father found hilarious. Then he said, "Now you're going to find out what parenthood is like. Now you'll understand about all the work and sacrifices."

Here we go again, I thought. By that point I was ill from whatever discount liquor my mother had been splashing in my glass. My parents had to help me to the old bed I'd slept in a few months—a lifetime—ago.

He doesn't get it, I said to myself, as I waited for the mattress to stop spinning. My father thought he was passing down the mantle of fatherhood like some precious Johnson heirloom. He didn't see that I'd be smashing our old patterns to make better ones. To start clean.

> *Our son Eric is a beautiful boy. He is intelligent and a real joy. I love him so much! I love Adrienne so much! I love this life!*
> —Dictionary entry, December 17, 1962

In quest of security, I took the city teacher's exam. The next February I became an art teacher at a junior high up in Washington Heights. When school let out, my day had just begun. I went to my education courses from four o'clock till seven, then hustled down to Columbus Avenue to tutor foreign-born students in English. (With the public schools paying $5,200 a year, we needed the extra cash.) At nine I hopped another train to teach an art class in Spanish Harlem, and then I went home.

My college graduation, once a barely imaginable milestone, passed without me. Already working toward my master's degree, I was too busy and nonconformist to bother tossing my cap in the air.

At age twenty-two, I had a wife, a child, a new apartment on the fashionable West Side, and a career in something important. Within two years I'd be chairman of the Art Department. I was even doing better with my father. We could talk about my job; I was rising in a world he'd experienced firsthand.

My course seemed set. No one could have foreseen that my nice, sure life was about to be upended.

Before tying the knot (that ominous phrase), as we flouted convention and the prevailing apartheid, Adrienne and I were the darlings of our college set. We were living our ideals. We would find our way, whatever it took.

But the fact remained that we were children, especially the groom. I was the dutiful son, born and bred. I did well to get into college and even better to get out. I honored my father and took care of my mother, two taxing assignments. Then came wife and baby and my trio of jobs, and I kept doing my duty each lockstep of the way. Though not afraid of hard work, I felt saddled and yoked, as entombed as old Perneb.

In theory, marriage held great appeal for me: two people wholly devoted, of like minds, indivisible. In practice, I had a problem: I wasn't ready to grow up.

My parents had raised a good, responsible boy with a shriveled sense of adventure. What they didn't realize was that brave new worlds came wrapped with fresh options. I made good, responsible choices, but I made them too soon; I'd veered from too many doors without knocking. Stretched out before me, straight and narrow as a yardstick, was a plod-along life in civil service. A sure life. A safe life.

My father's life, not mine.

I told myself that Adrienne had grown more conservative, less freewheeling. (Having a child, of course, will do that to you.) In 1963, when Eric was three years old, we split up. Adrienne wanted to keep trying, and I felt derelict in leaving my son. But I was also convinced that I had to go.

My mother said, "Nobody in our family has ever divorced." My father seconded her disappointment. But what did they know? Their marriage was a prison built for two, with no parole; they brought out the worst in each other. What stumped me was why they'd stuck it out so long.

Resorting to cliché, I told them I had fallen out of love. The reality was more damning. The truth was that I could not sustain love. For anyone.

Because something inside me was missing.

With my father entrenched at the post office and my mother with the city comptroller, they set their sights on a home of their own. It was amazing to see them work together so concertedly. My mother even drank less. She would sacrifice anything to escape Bed-Stuy.

I co-signed the mortgage and kicked in for the down payment, and in 1964 my parents joined the diaspora to Long Island. They settled in the black suburb of North Babylon, where my father registered Republican to appease the local bigwigs.

Their piece of the American dream was a brick-and-shingle three-bedroom on a corner lot—a modest house, but a veritable villa after what they'd had. When my mother surveyed her new estate—the two-car garage and deep backyard, the finished basement and shuttered

windows, the good used furniture from Aunt Marian—
she felt like a woman of means. The weary look she'd
worn in Brooklyn left her. Now she could be like the
other people in her office, no longer embarrassed to invite someone over.

As a nondriver, unfortunately, she also became more
isolated. There were no stores to walk to, and the commute was horrific. My mother had to be out with my father by five in the morning to get him to work by seven,
leaving two hours to kill before her shift. My father
waited on the other end, and they might not get home
till eight in the evening.

Despite their grind, they often baby-sat my son on the
weekends. It was a blessing for all concerned; Adrienne
needed relief, I needed support, and Eric thrived with the
attention. My mother spoiled him beautifully, as I knew
she would, and my father surprised me. He taught Eric to
box, took him bowling and to the movies. He was affec-
tionate and generous, showering the child with toys. He
even gave Eric his hallowed electric trains, the set he'd
confiscated away after my paint job.

I watched him with a jaundiced eye. With every good
deed, each tender glance and tolerant chuckle, my father
was expunging our past, a history he'd deny whenever I
felt moved to raise it. (*I never hit you,* he'd say, sounding
hurt. *You're making that up.*) He was wiping the slate,
which meant that he couldn't screw up, not once.

Rather than tilt me toward forgiveness, his kindness
embittered me the more. I saw his self-discipline with
Eric, his cool restraint, and what did that say about his
treatment of my mother and me?

When my parents moved, our gatherings moved with
them. All went well as long as the light held, while we
played ball or tag in the fenced-in yard. The stress

mounted after we came inside, when old enmities were poked at like embers in a campfire.

A spell of Guillain-Barré syndrome had forced Mama Tutt into an iron lung. For a year she was paralyzed from her toenails to her eyeballs, but she'd made a total comeback. Now fitted with a pacemaker, she was her feisty old self—if anything, the bid whist was rougher than ever. I'd pull Eric on my lap and partner my father; I liked helping him win because he was such a poor loser. If that meant cheating Mama Tutt, so be it, because she and Aunt Marian were cheating right back.

I would say, "Mama Tutt, I saw you point—"

And my loving grandmother would snarl, "Shut up!" When my side got on a hot streak and my father took to gloating, she would ball up her fists and sputter, "I'll get my boys from Chicago on you and kick your ass!"

I didn't wonder that Mama Tutt still despised my father, not after my mother answered the door one day with a bruise that defied makeup. But I didn't know then how deep the grudge ran. I wouldn't find out until recently, when my cousin Dianne divulged a secret that the women of our family had hoarded for generations.

Dianne was close to us growing up, and spent most of a summer on Gates Avenue when she was twelve. To this day she fondly recalls my mother's cooking, her assistance in sewing a dress.

Three years later, my cousin found herself alone with my father, who cornered and crudely propositioned her. In terror of her life, she got away and told her mother. Aunt Marian was devastated, but not surprised. My father, you see, had once made a pass at *her*.

They chose not to tell Uncle Syl, for his own protection. But they told Mama Tutt, and Dianne also took her story to my softhearted, empathetic mother.

Who called her a liar, and blamed the victim.

My cousin was traumatized. She never spoke of "Uncle

Jackie" after that. He was "Johnny's father," and she made sure not to be trapped again.

Through the years, I'd thought Mama Tutt a mite excessive in her threats against my father. When she'd mutter, "I oughta take a knife to him," I assumed it was the bourbon talking.

Now I see that she had sober grounds for homicide, or at least some amateur surgery. The old woman knew whom she was dealing with.

She had Black Jack's number from the start.

A year or so into my separation from Adrienne, I bumped into Laura Shapiro and brought her to a restaurant to catch up. After an hour of reminiscence, as the waiter poured coffee, she dropped her bombshell: "You know, your father was a real problem for us."

I nodded my understanding. Before we split up, Adrienne had complained about her father-in-law: "He scares me. He said some things to me that weren't right, and he scares me." When I went to my father, he zipped into his reflex denial: *Oh, no, I didn't do that. She's exaggerating—she's a white girl, she just misunderstood me. No, no, no* . . . It was awkward to press further, and I settled for putting him on notice.

According to Laura, however, the "problem" was worse than I'd feared. During our sophomore year at City College, when she'd been out to Gates Avenue with her roommate, John Sr. "made passes at us," she said. "He tried to feel us up. He came on to us when you were in another room. He did it with Adrienne, too."

There was more. My father ran down Laura's address through the post office. One evening he showed up at her building in Manhattan and buzzed her bell from the entry. When Laura told him to go away, he grudgingly relented.

The next time he somehow got *inside* the building

and made it all the way upstairs, to her door. He begged to be let in. (I could hear his hoarse whispers, his lewd entreaties.) Deathly afraid, Laura got rid of him only by threatening to call the cops.

She'd kept it from me, Laura explained, for fear of what I might do. "But your mother knew," my old girlfriend said, twisting the knife. "She had to know; I told her."

Dumbstruck, I felt the blood pulsing at my temples. I knew instantly that all that I'd heard was real. I flashed to how my father used to wink and leer at my girlfriends. I knew it then, I *knew* it, and I had put it away just as my mother put it away, because the truth gouged too deeply. I clung to the conviction that my family was good and decent, whatever our conflicts with one another.

Mom and Dad fine and sweet as ever . . .

But now I saw it was a lie. We had no principles, no loyalty. The Johnsons lived in a house of cards, and a wind had come to blow it down.

I paid the check and said goodbye to Laura. I walked to my garden apartment. I collected my dog, a Great Dane puppy named Kaiser Charlemagne, and crammed him into my Triumph two-seater.

I swung into the driver's seat and roared off to kill my father.

The night air and hour's drive would do nothing to allay me. The more time I had to mull Laura's story, the hotter I got. My father was the most jealous man I knew. He battered my mother and would have bludgeoned Emmett for a single date. Yet the same person had molested my sweethearts behind my back, might have raped them if he could. (And how better to wipe that college-boy smirk off my face?)

For too many years to count, I'd known my father as a domestic scoundrel, an in-house tormentor. But Laura had unmasked him as something more: an out-and-out criminal. I had to face it—my father was no good. He was the most depraved and remorseless individual to walk the earth. He stopped at nothing, drew no line.

I would have to draw one for him.

I flew out the Southern State Parkway to keep my appointment in Samarra. This was our third act. This was the way it had to be.

The trip passed in a blur, but I remember pulling up to my parents' house. I stomped up their stoop like a Hun sacking Rome. I punched the bell and dented the metal-framed storm door with my sneaker. I tromped back down to the yard, because you need elbow room to take someone apart.

Then I did something I had never done before. In a voice loud enough to wake the neighbors, I cursed my father: "Come on out, you son of a bitch!"

The inner door swung open to reveal a woman in her bathrobe behind the glass panel. My mother said, "What's wrong with you, Johnny?"

I spied a second figure in the shadows and said, "Tell him to come out of the house. I don't want to come in there and get him. I want him outside!"

When my father held back, I tagged him with all the dirty names I knew. I let loose my clotted anger from all the way back to Anacostia Flats. I cursed every time the bastard whipped me, even when I begged him not to; every mark on my mother's pretty face; each broken promise and random slap. I had stocked enough obscenities to last me a fortnight.

Finally he spoke up: "All right, I'm coming, but I got to get my jacket." As he fumbled with it, my mother latched on to him and blocked the door. "Let me out!" my father said, but he wasn't trying too hard to push past her.

From my gladiator's crouch I called, "Mama, let him out!"

My mother shrilled, "No, Johnny—don't, Jackie, *don't go out!*"

She was crying and I did not give a damn. I pointed at my father and said, "Why don't you just knock her down like you did before, *you no-good motherfucker!*"

At the peak of my patricidal fury, I glanced back at my car . . . and into the dilated eyes of Kaiser Charlemagne. My puppy was so young that his nose was still pink. He was trembling, in a lather. He saw his master going loco, and shared the emotion in triplicate.

I looked at my poor dog and thought, *What am I doing? It's not worth it. This guy is not worth killing.* The fight drained out of me. I looked back at my sniffling mother and said, "It's all right, Mom. It's okay."

"You were going to hit your father," she said.

"Well, I'm not going to hit him now," I said. "Why don't you come out here, Dad? I need to talk to you."

Sensing he was out of danger, my father joined me in the yard. I said, "Laura told me everything. How could you do this to your own son?"

"It's not true," he said. "That girl came on to me. She's exagger—"

"You're a liar," I said. "You told me not to lie, and now you lied about *this.* But you need to know one thing. I'll remember what you did to me. No matter what, I'll always remember."

I turned my back on him and took my puppy home.

I would like to tell you that my father became a nicer person in the wake of our face-off, that he found therapy or God or some old-fashioned shame. In fact, he never really changed. Though his chances would be fewer with my woman friends (whom I'd warn ahead of time), he would stay a lecher to his grave.

Yet something changed between us. Once he backed down, my father was the old emperor, a tin despot. He could wield the scepter at the head of his table, but we both knew it was papier-mâché. He could only run his bluff so far, for what if I snapped again?

As I cruised back to the city on that crazy, cathartic evening, with my grateful dog licking my face, I remember how glad I felt to be alive. I'd stepped away from the brink before doing something fatal.

I'd also come to a reckoning. From that point on, I would set my sails without weighing my father's approval. I'd withhold my love without guilt. I had not killed him, but he was dead inside me. I had broken my old man's hold at last.

And perhaps my mother's as well. When she harbored her husband in their doorway, the metaphor did not escape me. She was complicit; she had always been complicit. Having made her peace with a vampire, she would back him no matter what. Even if the quarry was her own precious child.

It was a hideous thought, but true: My parents deserved each other.

I didn't come around their house so often after that. I was no longer beholden. I was paid in full.

It is no coincidence, I think, that my life would be transformed over the next few years. By saying what I needed to my father, and moving on, I channeled violence into creative energy. I felt free and strong, and independent.

I would beat him my way, by showing who was the better man.

CHAPTER NINE

I will conclude with is this: I love my son, I failed him, I will try to do my best. I am no longer the [drama] merchant. Now I will work, use this book and try to love life!... Please forgive the sentimentalities of the writing. Goodbye dear dictionary.
— Dictionary entry, October 13, 1966

I'D ALWAYS HAD A WOMAN IN MY LIFE, FROM MOTHER TO WIFE, NOT a night in between. When I returned from Mexico with my divorce from Adrienne, my wife-to-be was waiting at the airport. Patsy was a former beauty queen, a willowy product of Main Line Philadelphia and the black upper middle class. We met when she was hired as a substitute teacher at J.H.S. 164, where I'd climbed to acting assistant principal.

In 1967, I left New York for a year as associate professor at my wife's alma mater, Lincoln University, a black college outside Philadelphia. My duties were to paint and guest-lecture, which left lots of time for our newborn daughter, Cydney. After Washington Heights, Lincoln felt like a sabbatical. Best of all, I was far from the messy tangle of my parents' lives.

Indiana University accepted me into its predoctoral program in art history. I bought a used green Cadillac. Life was good.

Then my best-laid plans took a hard left turn. After writing for an anthology called *Black Power Revolt,* I was asked to speak to the Overseas Press Club in New York. I took my shot to critique the media coverage of the inner-city uprisings. My audience included Steve Fleischman, a staunch liberal and executive producer for long-form documentaries at ABC.

Young black talent was a hot commodity at the time. A week or so later, Steve's department offered me a field production job, despite the fact that I'd never made so much as a home movie.

It was a fat opportunity, and a huge gamble. I was thirty years old, a footloose kid no longer. I'd be risking a lifetime sinecure in academe for a thirteen-week contract, sink or swim. Maybe that's why I took the job, because I'd tired of playing safe and doing the expected. With my feet planted firmly in midair, I moved my family back to New York and—*shazam!*—found myself on a special on urban ecology with Sidney Poitier.

I learned as I went, using my art background to compose our camera shots. Documentaries were in vogue, and my thirteen-week apprenticeship became a three-year hitch as producer, director, and writer. Here was the medium I'd loved since those Saturdays at Loew's. Each day brought new adventure. I was having the time of my life.

It wasn't quite so much fun for Patsy, I'm afraid, as work stole me away for long stretches. With the arrival of our twins, Anthony and Christina, she had three children to tend to (plus Eric on the weekends) as a virtually single mom. When we filmed *To All the World's Children,* a

sprawling study of UNICEF and hunger, I spent ten con-
secutive months in Africa, Asia, and South America, with
but a single stopover in New York. I missed my family, of
course. But I'd been handed a new career, and how could
I let it go? By the time the job was finished, the twins
would cry when I held them. They did not know who I
was.

I assuaged my guilt by living frugally on the road and
handing most of my expense allowance to Patsy. I stayed
faithful as a monk, wrote my wife five times a week. I
pined like a family man should.

In honesty, however, I felt most myself in the field. The
more remote the destination, the better. When I sat in my
hut in Kenya, warding off malaria with quinine and gin, I
was impregnable. I was free from the pain of relationship. And as the night fell black and silent, I would wonder: Was my father more committed to family than I? Did
he love me more than I loved my children?

When I came home for postproduction, I was a real
parent. I played with my kids, organized dinner and bath-
time. After a week or two, though, I began to feel smothered again—by my marriage and my in-laws, and
especially by my parents. It was hard to ignore the latest
news flash: my mother's weekend bender, my father's
screaming fit. I couldn't just shut them out, not after
Grandpa and Grandma had helped so while I was MIA.

My parents and I were characters in different movies.
A visit meant leaving *La Dolce Vita* for my scenes in
some hamfisted farce, and I couldn't stop thinking that
I'd been badly miscast. As I stepped through the door in
North Babylon, I'd be felled by lethargy. I was slogging
through the mud of my past.

Holidays were the worst. On Christmas my mother
sipped her bourbon and burned the biscuits. When I
asked her not to drink in front of the children, she got offended. My father tortured Mama Tutt. My mother drank

some more and Shuffled off to Buffalo. My father held forth on NATO when he couldn't even spell it. I simmered till I boiled, and then we left. My favorite time was in the car back to the city, when my family slept and I could drive in quietude.

I did no better at home. After we finished with the kids at night, and Patsy passed out from exhaustion, the walls of our cozy West Side brownstone—complete with washer-dryer—closed in on me. I felt trapped in a middle-class cul-de-sac, and by eleven I'd be fishing for my keys. Better an arrested adolescence than none at all, I figured. I'd tiptoe out the door like Daddy Jekyll after his phosphorescent cocktail, to become: Night Crawler Hyde!

The hippest scene in New York in the late 1960s and early 1970s was Max's Kansas City, on Park Avenue and 18th Street. Frequented by Jane Fonda and Jimi Hendrix, it broke ground by posting a doorman to decide who might enter. I wasn't too jaded (or so many years removed from Gates Avenue) to feel a rush, each time, at being ushered through the magic gateway.

Inside, the joint would be pulsing with laughter and the Rolling Stones. Greeting my friends at the big table at the front, I'd feel like a drowning man come up for air. As the bar tab soared, the company kept getting wittier. We'd go at it till closing, when I'd wend my way home and fall into bed. After a few hours' rest, I'd get up with the kids and be off to my job across from Lincoln Center.

The marriage sort of fell by the wayside. Patsy had her problems, too, with her own sticky family background, and our union was troubled from the start. My second go-round befuddled me as much as my first, or more so, as my children now numbered four. I came into family life with a blank blackboard. My mom taught me that wedlock was a death trap; my dad, that fathers ate their young. It was easy to reject their models, harder to find good alternatives.

I proceeded by trial and error, and more error. The surface rituals of marriage came easy, but its depths eluded me. I'd be sauntering along in sweet normalcy—wrestling with a child's socks, making small talk over eggs with my wife—and suddenly I'd feel like Camus' stranger.

What was I doing here, and why?

When Frank Reynolds called in sick one morning, I went on-camera for a show on the West Virginia coal miners. Gunning for my first big interview, I chased union boss Tony Boyle into a federal courtroom, where I promptly got arrested.

My grit won me a raise and a new job: network correspondent, based in New York. On September 9, 1971, a slow-news Thursday, the assignment editor asked me to check out "a little prison disturbance" outside Buffalo. It wasn't a big deal, he said, but I'd get some useful seasoning. No need to bring a change of clothes; I'd be there and back the same day.

I could tell that we'd miscalculated as soon as I reached the Attica Correctional Facility. The inmates had taken forty-two guards hostage and ruled much of the interior. Knots of hard-eyed locals stood outside the high gray wall. The state corrections commissioner, Russell G. Oswald, had landed to put out the fire, with Governor Nelson Rockefeller keeping close tabs. National media heavyweights were alighting en masse—*whoa,* wasn't that Robert Shackney, ace correspondent for CBS News?

I had been dropped into the biggest story in the Western world. Aided only by a cameraman, I'd be filing for national and local television *and* radio. My hotel was an hour away. As I needed a telephone for my radio spots and to reach my editors, I'd have to rely on the kindness of strangers.

Attica was a classic penitentiary town. The prison staff was predominantly white, the inmates more than three-

quarters black and Puerto Rican. Dark people were sus-
pect. After watching other reporters trot into a house
across the street to use the phone, I asked the owner for
the same favor. He looked at me dourly and said, "No, *you*
can't come in here." I wound up sprinting to a redneck
bar blocks away, where the proprietor sullenly let me use
his pay phone.

Late that first afternoon, I was picked to join Oswald
and a few other journalists for his first talks with the inmates. Tape recorder in hand, I followed the commissioner through the arched doorway at the turreted main
gate. We quietly formed a double line and filed into the
administration building, still under the state's control.
After passing through two more gates, we entered A
Block, no-man's-land.

At the next gate our armed escorts fell back, passing
us on to the other side: half a dozen large men, masked
and turbaned like Bedouins. Only their eyes were visible
through towels and sweatshirts, and what I saw there—
less anger than a hard resignation—unnerved me. As we
trailed them down a low corridor, the flash point of the
insurrection, a throng of hooting inmates pressed in on
either flank. Some brandished makeshift knives or baseball bats.

I was scared. To judge by his shallow breathing and
the beads of sweat on his forehead, so was Oswald. The
commissioner was short and round, with thinning hair
and a jowly, freckled face. He looked like a guy who ran
a thriving Buick dealership in Tulsa.

He looked, I feared, like a man way out of his depth.

Two checkpoints later, we saw daylight at the end of
our tunnel. We walked to its edge . . . and stepped into
the pandemonium of D Yard.

I will never forget that tableau. More than a thousand
maximum-security prisoners milled about, exalting in

their newfound freedom. For shelter from the elements, they'd built a tent city out of bed frames and mattresses.

At the center of the yard, fifty yards or so from the tunnel, long tables were laid end to end for the parlay. To go forward was like entering the Colosseum—as the featured act. A security team linked arms to form a human chain and divide us from the at-large population, now massing ten and twelve deep. With Oswald leading our parade, we were buffeted by jeers and threats and epithets. We were the enemy. Our fate was a tactical question.

Get outta the way! Let the bastards through!
Ought to keep you guys in here, you racist pigs!
No, man, we've given our word—leave 'em alone!

I glanced to my right and spotted a whitish man who seemed out of place. Thinking he might be a hostage, I looked away. I didn't want to see anything I wasn't supposed to.

Then I heard a voice that stopped me short: *John! Got to help us, John, man! These pigs want to kill us! Hey, John!* I looked up at a dark-skinned guy about my age; I knew him by sight from the old neighborhood. The flashback was unsettling, surreal.

Within a swelling clamor, I took my seat at the far end of the tables, where my cameraman could get a good angle on Oswald. The inmate negotiating committee, a row of stern-looking black men, sat opposite with their backs to the brick facade of D Block. Behind us crushed a throng of semi-liberated humanity. There would be no exit unless they gave us one.

With a stunning lack of savoir faire, the commissioner proposed a surrender, loosing a new hail of threats from the crowd. A sizable faction seemed ready to take us hostage. *Don't incite them,* I muttered. Oswald's lips were trembling. The Buick dealer's demo had stalled at a train crossing, with the engine so close he could feel the rails hum.

The tumult subsided. Given their chance to be heard, the inmate leaders weren't about to blow it. They spoke of the slave labor at Attica, of the rotten food and health care. They charged that several guards belonged to a local Klan-type organization, and that prisoners were punished for no reason but their color.

"We are men!" declared L. D. Barkley, a twenty-one-year-old firebrand in granny glasses who'd been locked up for forging a money order. "We are not beasts and we do not intend to be beaten or driven as such. . . . What has happened here is but the sound before the fury of those who are oppressed."

Though I doubted it made much difference to Oswald, we were dealing with some very smart, very eloquent people. I was bowled over by their analysis, because I knew it to be correct. Regardless of what they had or hadn't done, these prisoners lived in a system that took everything from them, starting with their dignity. Unlike the honchos at my network, I had tasted their frustration. The inmates were right. They were *right*.

As Oswald dithered in response, I recognized another Bed-Stuy alumnus, a slight man with a scruffy beard. Before I left, he approached me and said, "John, if I don't get out of here, tell my mother that I was doing the right thing." He spoke as if he were already dead. And I thought: *How was it that I came to be on one side of the wall, and this man on the other?*

The session lasted forty-five minutes without combusting. Tethered to our security team, Oswald and the rest of us walked out without a scratch. Those phenomenal inmate leaders had everything under control.

Even then I sensed that Attica would end badly. It was obvious that the governor faced more than a mere riot. He was dealing with a politicized group, with a *rebellion,* and its upshot overran the prison gate. To right the wrongs inside would mean facing what was wrong outside, in society, and nobody was prepared to do that.

The entire press corps debriefed me, a coup for ABC. Over the next four days, working with no relief and next to no sleep, on a diet of coffee and sugar donuts, I would file a total of ninety-five reports.

As the siege continued, tensions rose. I met growing hostility when I tried to speak with hostage families. By Sunday, September 12, talks had stalled. Oswald ruled out any amnesty, creating a hopeless impasse.

That evening I saw more people gather by the wall, a bunch of tight-faced white guys with guns. None were in uniform, though quite a few sported badges. Were they off-duty guards? Local cops? Simple citizens on the prowl?

Rockefeller ran out of patience. Snipers with big-game rifles were dispatched to roofs overlooking D Yard. Other units, armed with pistols and shotguns, were stationed in the tunnels and on the catwalks.

I called my producer in Buffalo and said, "It's going to happen soon." I called my mother, who begged me to be careful. She was really afraid for me; she had a feeling that I wouldn't come back.

The morning of Monday, September 13, dawned drizzly and cold. I knew it was over when I heard the helicopters, just before ten o'clock. The people around me donned their gas masks. I had nothing.

The chopping got louder, closer; the concussion shook the ground. I thought, *It must feel like this in Vietnam, but this time we're killing our own.* The raid was on. Enshrouded in a cloud of CS gas, I fell to my knees. My lungs seized up; my eyes were wet holes of pain. Struggling back to my feet, I propped myself against the concrete wall. Through the toxic fog I made out forms in yellow rain gear. They were charging through the gate, weapons drawn.

They would have their sport. My ears were hammered by a deafening fusillade, the sound of 2,000 rounds fired in a span of six minutes.

As the shooting grew sporadic, I beheld a scene that would haunt me forever: a stream of savages bolting out of Attica with blood on their hands. Screaming in panic, they ripped off their masks and hurled away their guns before scattering in every direction. I moved from the wall to dodge the traffic. Then I saw him—fortyish, sandy-haired, tan uniform—running straight at me. His rifle was pointed at the center of my chest.

"Don't shoot!" I said. "Don't shoot! Don't shoot! *Don't shoot!*"

The cop roared, *"Nigger-nigger-nigger-nigger!"* His eyes were wild, his face glazed with sweat. He came close enough to bayonet me—and then he dashed on past, threw down his gun, and kept running into the sunset.

I staggered about, legally blind, until some Good Samaritan dabbed ointment on my eyes. My vision cleared enough for me to wobble to a press conference by the main gate. I heard Oswald claim victory while other officials drummed the Rockefeller line: that several hostages had their throats slashed in "cold-blooded killings" by the inmates.

I found my cameraman and filmed at the wall. I was dazed from lack of sleep, heaving from the gas, reeling from the bombardment, and spooked by my near-death encounter. But I believe that I conveyed the emotions of the moment:

> It's an awful thing. . . . I think that people are dying in there, and it seems— [At that point I cut and tried again.] Helicopters are flying right overhead. There was an announcement from the helicopter right above me to the in-

mates below that they should put their hands
on their heads and come out. . . . I'm upset.
This is unfortunate what has happened here.
And whatever happens after the situation
here at Attica, the penal system in the United
States, and the people who are kept inside,
will never be the same.

ABC killed that piece, though years later it would be
used in the documentary *Eyes on the Prize, Part II.* By
the end of it I was jabbing my mike at the camera like an
angry index finger, which my bosses deemed unprofes-
sional. I'd made no mention of the slashings or a rumored
castration. Whose side was I on?

Arriving belatedly on the scene, my producer brought
new marching orders: back to our Buffalo affiliate for a
live report. On the way I threw up in the car. I was still
woozy entering the studio, and I knew that I looked a
mess. When asked about the inmate "atrocities," reported
elsewhere pretty much as fact, I demurred. I had been
trained to report what I'd seen, what I *knew,* and to be
skeptical of spoon-fed hearsay. No journalist had exam-
ined any bodies. No doctor had appeared at the press
conferences.

The men I'd met inside were too adroit to kill their
hostages. Why would they throw away their only lever-
age and protection?

The next day, the Monroe County medical examiner
concluded that all nine hostages who died in the siege
were killed by gunshot wounds—by friendly fire. In con-
firming those findings, a top pathologist added that a
number of dead inmates, including L. D. Barkley, had been
shot in the back.

The facts weren't enough to save my career at ABC,
however. Before Attica I was perceived as a bright young
man on the rise. After Attica I was the rookie who had

blown the big story. Important people at the network mistrusted my smarts and skills, and most of all my "objectivity" as a black person.

Maybe they were right. I felt that I understood Attica for what it was: a state-sanctioned massacre. Thirty-two inmates were slaughtered there, and hundreds more wounded. Uncounted others were tortured in the immediate aftermath of the raid, when the cops took their revenge. Inmates were stripped naked, forced to crawl through the mud, burned with cigarettes, and beaten about their genitals. Patients fresh from surgery were clubbed unconscious. When asked about these incidents, Oswald called them a "fraternity hazing."

The toll was not abstract to me. I knew those men across the table, whether or not I'd grown up with them. I could not accept the official reasons for the raid. Why didn't the governor wait? The inmates were running out of food—where were they going to go? Were black lives so cheap, after all?

Patsy would say that I changed after my sojourn to upstate New York. My old optimism now seemed like naïveté. I got tougher and a little meaner. My dark side—my distanced, callused, unreachable side—came to the fore.

A part of me never made it out of Attica alive.

CHAPTER TEN

ON MY FIRST DAY ON THE JOB AT WABC, THE LOCAL STATION where I'd found safe harbor, the news director asked my name. When I told him, he said, "No, your real name."

"That's it—John Johnson."

"Then we're going to have to change it, you know."

"I don't want to change it. I'm John Johnson, and I want to stay John Johnson."

"Well," he said, unable to hide his disappointment, "I guess we'll have to try and work with it."

A saner man would have walked and kept on going, but I had crossed the Rubicon. I'd quit the network and gone over to its New York flagship, getting a raise in the process. Back in 1972, *Eyewitness News* was hot and rising in the New York City market, a pioneer in up-close-and-personal TV journalism. Its headliners included Geraldo Rivera, who'd made his name by exposing medieval conditions at the state mental hospital at Willowbrook.

I began as a street reporter on the early morning shift, picking up the overnight murders. As I got smoother and faster, I moved to better stories. Over the next several years, I exposed the Medellín drug cartel's penetration

into the city's streets, and helped shut down an abusive
foster care center on Staten Island. In hostage situations
I became the gunman's mediator of choice. After I rescued an altar boy in Harlem and a prison guard in New
Jersey, my star was rising once more.

Cashing in, WABC hyped me with a spot to spin Ed-
ward R. Murrow in his grave: *John Johnson doesn't just
report the news, he helps make it!* I joined the regulars
at Elaine's, my mug shot posted with the rest of salon royalty. I'd get stopped for autographs at Bloomingdale's. My
local Q score rivaled Walter Cronkite's. When I attended
the third Ali–Norton fight in Yankee Stadium, I sat between Jack Dempsey and Mick Jagger.

Though I'd theoretically taken the job to spend more
time with my family, I was working harder than ever. I
was one hell of a provider, and an all-star father when I
happened to be around. But Patsy and I both knew the
marriage was failing. We divorced when Cydney was
eight and the twins six.

As a weekend single dad, I was a natural. I took the kids
to parties in the Hamptons or on vacations with my girlfriend of the moment. We had great fun. I let them stay up
late and cooked breakfast to order the next morning.

I wanted my children to love me—no, it was more
than that. I wanted their forgiveness.

How simple it had been for my father! Good behavior
was good (and expected); bad was bad, which meant a
slap upside my head. For me, by contrast, parenting was
a maze of cul-de-sacs. When my children tested me, I tem-
porized. I equivocated. I hoped to be their friend, which
meant I gave away the store.

Although I'd inherited my father's hot temper, I never
touched Eric in anger. The younger ones got a rare swat
on the rump, no more. Even so, there were times when I
scared myself. I remember one dinner where Anthony
crossed the line and I imploded, grabbing the pot of

mashed potatoes and slamming it on the table. I stared down the sorry offender and ordered him into the bedroom, the closest thing I had to a woodshed.

But the spanking never happened. I was stopped short by the startled looks on those small faces, jerking up at me like puppies on a leash. At their age I'd lived in fear all the time, till it was part of my inner landscape. From what I knew of George Johnson, I'd have bet that my father lived there, too. I'd heard all about those cycles, how abuse got passed on like a bad gene.

But not in this family. The ugly pattern, I vowed, would be laid to rest. It would stop with me.

My father took people for granted, including the woman he woke up to. It wouldn't occur to him to bring her flowers, or slip her a few dollars for a dress, or spring for an anniversary dinner. When my mother's birthday neared, I shopped for my dad's gift as well as my own, just in case.

My mother had long resigned herself to her husband's neglect. It was as if her marriage came in a closeout sale: no returns, no exchanges. But at some point in the late 1970s, when she was nearly sixty, her patience wore through. He had beaten her again, and she'd had enough. She stayed briefly with her family before moving to my apartment. I gave her the bedroom and took the pullout couch.

The visit was a disaster. My new roommate came to me depressed, and dulled her pain by swigging my pricey Burgundies. When I got home from work, she'd saved a hundred questions about my day. My mother was too big a character in my book, and soon I was exhausted.

I knew that she hoped I would ask her to move in for good. When the offer didn't come, she sensed felt rejected. Since nobody loved her, she said, she might as well go back to Jackie.

I didn't try to change her mind. I felt selfish, but I knew she'd go back to him eventually no matter what I said. She might dislike my father at times, but she would always be tied to him. For all the meanness in their marriage, neither one could break free of it.

After my mother returned home, her complaints redoubled. She began mentioning her lunches with a fellow named Joe, a co-worker in the comptroller's office. I asked her, "Does he like you?"

My mother said, "We like each other, and he's very nice to me."

"Have you gone out with him?"

"Only for lunch—we don't have any place to go."

I pictured the sad, aging woman at the other end of the line, and I said, "Well, if you need some place to bring him, you can use my apartment."

My offer was half-serious, and I was jolted when she took me up on it. This wasn't some randy fraternity brother. How could I lend my own mother a love nest?

Perhaps I knew her too well. My mother played the *grande dame* to the world, but she couldn't fool her old drinking buddy. I saw through to the fears that defeated her, to her hunger for attention. I knew of my father's many affairs and his idiotic jealousy. I guess I figured that he had it coming.

To establish her alibi, my mother told him she'd be working late one night, and that it would be easier to stay over with me. She arrived at my door with a small suitcase and a skinny Italian man. "This is Joe," she said. As we shook hands, I towered over him.

I had never seen my mother act this way before: nervous and edgy, but also aglow. She looked beautiful, which made the setup more tawdry. I mumbled my goodbye and left for my girlfriend's house. The next day, when my mother thanked me, I changed the subject.

There would be four or five trysts at my apartment, as

I recall. When I went to North Babylon and my father lapsed into his macho man routine, my mother and I would share a knowing glance, a silent snicker. After all these years, we'd outwitted the old fool. We had gotten the last laugh.

For my mother, though, the affair was more than one-upmanship. She seemed subtly different at home, above the fray. She had carved out a space where her ego didn't rest on my father's favor.

Yet even as she blossomed, I couldn't shake my dis-comfort. I had no illusions about my parents' marriage, but did I need to be a party to their cheating? It was wrong on every level, and I pulled the plug. If my mother wanted to continue seeing Joe, she would have to do it elsewhere. With that, I believe, the business ended.

Or maybe it didn't, at least for me. The fact of the mat-ter was this: I had betrayed my father. In an oblique way, I had taken my mother from him. I knew it would kill him if he found out, as surely as putting a .45 to his head. I had fixed him, but good.

My father never did find out. After decades of baseless suspicions, he stayed in the dark the one time my mother strayed. And so we got away with it, which is not to say we were untouched. We'd become *too* close, too inti-mate. I stopped short of gouging my eyes out, like my Greek forerunner, but I avoided my mother's touch. I found excuses not to dance with her and held back from her hugs. We were unclean, the both of us, and only time could lift the stain.

In the 1980s everything accelerated. I had my own in-vestigative unit at WABC and then co-anchored the evening and nightly news with Bill Beutel. I won eight local Emmys, four in a single year.

I rented a loft in the heart of SoHo with ample room for my artwork. My studio was so huge, in fact, that I ran laps there with my personal trainer. If I wasn't working, running, painting, or sleeping, I was dining at a power table at Le Cirque, or clubbing into the night at Xenon or Aria, or passing through the velvet rope at Studio 54, the ultimate adult theme park.

If excess was the zeitgeist of the 1980s, no one was more in tune with it than I. I could not do enough, have enough, *be* enough. For years I had a sporadic affair with a notorious, doomed blond actress—our little secret, until we were outed on the cover of *Paris Match*.

Adrienne was the second woman I'd ever slept with, and Patsy the fourth. Now I made up for lost time. At one point I was seeing three local anchorwomen, a state official, a city official, a hatcheck girl, a network producer, and various models, reporters, and executive secretaries. There were times when I'd enter the elevator at the *Eyewitness News* building and be stumped at which button to push. There were four floors, and I had something going with a woman on every one.

I was a man in full bloom, and I regret not a minute of it.

Meanwhile, out on Long Island, an aging couple charted their boy's progress in astonishment. My parents thought I'd made it as a public school administrator. They preened when I moved to Lincoln University. They busted their buttons when the network aired my documentaries.

But when I became a face on *Eyewitness News,* the Johnsons won the Lotto. My parents had only to turn on the television (which was on all the time, anyway, since my father had retired) and there was Little Johnny Boy beaming into their home twice a night, my big old head filling the screen.

My mother basked in the neighbors' inquiries, in the attention shown her—*How are* you *today, Mrs. Johnson?*—at the A&P. I called her religiously after each show, as eager as a boy in his grammar school pageant: Did she see me? How did I look? How did I do? Her reviews were distinctly maternal:

"That was really good, and you looked great in that suit."

Or, "Well, you looked a little tired, but that was a wonderful story."

Or, "You need to comb your hair and fix that messy head of yours, boy!"

My father rarely took the phone. For John Sr. my success was double-edged. He wanted me to do well, of course, yet couldn't help resenting me. In his mind we were playing a zero-sum game. The bigger I got, the smaller he felt.

It didn't help that my stature was rubbed in his face. When I came to a family get-together, I was treated with pomp and circumstance. I couldn't remove my jacket before my mother prompted, "Well, Johnny, what do you want?" My aunt and grandmother gushed along in chorus.

My father would protest, "How come you ask him before me?" but no one heard him. They might serve his dinner first to duck a riot, but they'd do it offhandedly, like a coffee shop girl at the end of her shift. When Aunt Marian placed her hand on my shoulder and gently slid my food in front of me, the distinction was clear. Under her breath, she'd say, *Your father wishes he were like you.*

My father and I both doted on chicken gizzards, and he would check my plate to see that I didn't get more than my share. Just before dinner one evening, my mother called me to the kitchen and wrapped all the gizzards in a slice of white bread. I wolfed them on the spot.

When my father was served a few minutes later, he glared down and said, "Irene, there's no gizzards in this chicken!"

"No," my mother said, "the butcher must have taken them out."

My days of deference were done; I claimed center stage as my due. Puffed up by the women's praise, I'd gently contradict my father's take on Gorbachev or Arafat: "Maybe you ought to look at it in a different way." After all, I had been to the Balkans and Jerusalem, to the Bush retreat in Kennebunkport. In time I would accompany Nelson Mandela on his maiden trip to a voting booth. I *knew* what I was talking about.

My father argued halfheartedly until my mother interrupted: "Why don't you listen to your son? You don't read anything, anyway. How can you have an opinion if you don't even read the newspaper?" She'd become more openly subversive, rolling her eyes or sucking her incisors when annoyed.

My father groused that we were all in league against him, but his complaints were pro forma. The old lion had lost his teeth. He could no longer outrun me or outfight me, or even out-talk me. The future belonged to Junior.

Yet my victory seemed hollow. Long before they grew old and sick, my parents were a burden to me. Their relationship had not mellowed with age. If anything, as my mother grew bolder, the wrangling got worse. Each night between my news shows, I refereed their spats over the phone. Battle fatigue set in. Many were the weekends when I raced out to the Hamptons for some R&R, zooming past my parents' exit with a mix of release and remorse.

When I couldn't avoid it, I took a deep breath and dove into the split-level home. Before long I'd be bailing outside to their stoop, regardless of the weather, a fugitive from my own people.

I'd count the minutes till I could pack up my headache and flee. My friends and girlfriends, brought along for insulation, would say, "Gee, I wish I had parents like yours.

You can talk with them about anything." I could not explain why I was such a wreck when we left. Or abrupt and prickly for days afterward, like the man whose name was my name, too.

I'd bring my parents whenever I was honored by a civic group or professional association. I thanked them in every acceptance speech. I thought it only fair; the awards were theirs as much as mine.

My father handled these events with aplomb. As for my mother . . . well, my mother was a basket case. When I tried to calm her, she'd be affronted: *Don't fuss with me, now!* But I wasn't being critical. I just wanted her to take it easy and be herself.

One day I was hosting WABC's *Morning Show,* live from the studio, and they brought her on as a surprise guest. When someone asked her a question, she sat paralyzed, eyes darting like pinballs. I had to laugh—"Oh, Mom"—and I gave her a hug. It became a sweet, if less than informative, television moment. (My father zinged his wife that night: *"Huh,* she runs her mouth in the house all the time, and then she can't say a damn thing when it counts!")

Some time later, the station arranged to pick her up after work for a Mother's Day spot. The date loomed like the Inquisition. Fear-stricken that she'd freeze again, she downed a triple vodka before the crew's arrival. By the time the tape rolled, my mother was snockered, and this time I wasn't there to save her.

What was your son's favorite song as a child?

Her brow furrowed in concentration. Then a grateful smile appeared, and she said, "He used to love to sing, 'Jesus Loves Me.'"

Could you sing it for us?

In a tremulous mezzo she began, "Jesus loves me, yes I know; 'Cause the Bible tells me sooo . . ." She finished the verse and stopped cold, looking spent and slightly addled.

When I tuned in with my family on Sunday, I was mortified. *My mother, the lush*—God knows how many people had their stereotypes confirmed that afternoon. My father made a cruel joke. My grandmother said, "Irene, why would you do that? You embarrassed all of us."

My mother was devastated. Her big opportunity—her chance to express to all how she felt about me—had backfired. While I felt for her, I wished that I could use my aunt as a standby mom in public.

A few years later, when they taped my dad for a Father's Day special, he was the model of poise. No, he said, I was never any trouble as a child; I was always a good boy. When I saw the program, I misted up. I barely winced when he shared his parenting technique: *Spare the rod and spoil the child . . .*

Those two vignettes revealed my parents in their differences—the one a bundle of garish insecurities, the other as smooth and cool as granite. My mother was smarter than my father, and wiser, but she was no match for his self-possession. Then again, masters tend to have more confidence than slaves.

I liked it when my father fed the assumption that I hailed from the middle class. I wasn't one to blab about my humble beginnings. I wanted to be accepted for my work, not as some model bootstrap boy. My father had that elusive quality known as class, and I was grateful.

On the other hand, I had dedicated my adulthood to being all that my father was not. I aimed to be kind where he was wicked, giving where he was stingy, worldly where he was parochial and unread. And now, all these years later, I was . . . a chip off the old block! The apple fallen close to the tree! Friends would pay me tribute—*You're just like your dad*—and I'd chafe at the comparison.

Was I indeed my father's son? Did the legacy run deeper than my foot speed or the shape of my hands?

The question dogged me, most of all in my romantic life. I was undeniably drawn to "nice" women with high morals, even as I flitted about town like a middle-aged refugee from the Summer of Love.

A double standard, any way you cut it.

Where my father tyrannized, I chose the other path: detachment. As a girlfriend once said, "Loving you is like loving smoke." Even when physically present (and I fear this was true with my children as well), I was never completely there. A part of me stayed at a safe remove. My bags were always packed.

I made it clear that I could care for myself, and sooner or later the women in my life got the message: *I don't need you.* Compulsively generous, I was lousy at receiving. As a child I'd come by love and pain from the same bedeviled source, and I still confused the two. I pulled back at the most intimate times. I'd been hurt more deeply than I might admit; I did not want to be hurt again.

As my mother's martyrdom attested, commitments were dangerous things. They could leave you snared and abandoned, wounded for all time. Worse, they might impel you to wound another. In one of my less stable relationships, a woman slapped me in a heated argument. I saw red and grabbed her by the throat with both hands—until I saw the terror in her face. It was my mother's face, and who did that make me?

I let go in a flash. Sick with self-loathing, I apologized every which way. Even after the woman forgave me, I could not forgive myself. I could only make sure that it never happened again.

As part of a report on professional boxing, I interviewed Floyd Patterson at his home in upstate New York. To get some action on tape, we sparred a few rounds in his gym. I was forty-four years old and in fair enough shape; Floyd was forty-eight, but his rippled torso seemed stuck at twenty-seven.

The sparring went well. I looked every inch an intramural middleweight champion, give or take a quarter-century. I looked so good, in fact, that the New York Firefighters Burn Center Foundation carded Floyd and me as the main event at its annual fund-raiser: three rounds at the Felt Forum.

It seemed like a terrific idea at the time. To help sell the attraction, I did a silly little promo on my station: "Come to Madison Square Garden on Thursday, April 14, and watch me knock Floyd Patterson out!"

On the appointed evening, to fanfares from *Rocky,* I burst into the packed arena in a crimson robe with "WABC" on my back. As I waved to my parents sitting ringside, I nearly missed Floyd's simple entrance: a towel around his neck, black trunks, all business. He wasn't smiling as he had been upstate. I might have been paranoid, but he didn't seem quite so friendly.

After we met at center ring, and the ref droned through his pre-fight litany, Floyd looked at me and said, "These people have paid good money, so we've got to put on a big show. I don't know why you did that promo, but you better protect yourself."

By the time I collected my jaw from the canvas, Floyd had moved off and turned his massive back to me. I retreated to my own corner, the jaunt gone from my step. They weren't playing *Rocky* anymore. Was Floyd serious? Was he planning to box for real?

The bell rang, and my opponent lumbered back out to meet me, bigger than life—*Floyd Patterson,* two-time heavyweight champion of the world. His blank face promised no dispensation. It hit me that it was hubris to be here without headgear, not to mention a two-by-four and a Rottweiler.

Stick and move, stick and move . . . I danced my way

through the first round. When I landed a harmless punch on Floyd's arm, it was like slamming a tree stump; I tingled up to my elbow. After a three-minute eternity, I shuffled back to my stool, grateful not to need a cut man. My teenaged son, Anthony, was unimpressed. "Do something!" he urged. "You've got to do something!"

I looked at him and said, "Are you *crazy?*"

In the second round I connected with a lucky jab, and Floyd countered with a left to my rib cage—*phoom!*—and a pile-driving right to the solar plexus—*phuhh!* It was an amazing sensation, from the initial jolts to the pain that radiated from my scalp to my toes. It hurt so much that I dropped my arm to shield my abdomen from the next blow, leaving myself wide open for a left hook: Floyd's knockout punch. I braced myself for the crash, but it never came. Maybe Floyd took mercy on my overmatched ass. Or maybe he chose to keep the match going as a gesture to the paying customers.

Answering the bell for the third round, I felt a weird sense of calm. Riding into the valley of death, with nothing more to lose, I relaxed. I used everything in my arsenal and even landed a sweet left-right to the center of Floyd's forehead. When the final bell rang, my opponent smiled at me and said, "Good show!" I came out of it with a swollen right eye, my badge of honor, but no internal injuries. All things considered, Floyd had been very kind.

Sweat pouring off me, I hopped down to embrace my teary mother and ecstatic aunt. I gave my father a gentle hug, instead of our usual mock headlock. He gaped at me and said, "You looked real good in there."

It was then that I knew the reason I'd chanced life and limb. It was for him. *Pop that jab,* he'd once told me, *with your hand like the end of a whip.* The best lessons were often the old ones, and my father had taught me well.

There was no tension in the smoky air that night, no

rivalry between us. My dad was glowing with a mentor's pure pride. "Imagine, my son in the ring with Floyd Patterson," he'd say for weeks afterward. "That Johnny Boy is something, man. He is *something*."

It was funny. Coming from him, I could almost believe it.

In May 1987, I eloped with a former Miss Cheerleader USA from Indiana, a blond and brainy free spirit. In E. Jean I met my match. An emergent writer and TV personality, she was no less driven and tempestuous than I. Our defining moment came when I stomped on her grandmother's hand-sewn quilt, a tantrum later immortalized by E. Jean in the pages of *Esquire*.

I was wound tighter than a drum. I'd tried to be all things to all people—son, father, husband, globe-trotting newsman, downtown *boulevardier*—until I was snowed under. I had ex-wives calling and grown children struggling, and I rafted along with the tide, grabbing what spare time I could for my art. The wonder was that my third marriage lasted as long as it did, just over three years.

I counted myself an enlightened spouse. When in town I did most of the shopping and cooking; I wanted to be supportive of E. Jean's career. But I was kidding myself. What I really wanted was a traditional helpmate, a woman who would pack my bags and ferry me to the airport, and be there when I came back. A wife who would plot her life around my needs.

A girl just like the girl, in short, who'd married dear old dad.

CHAPTER ELEVEN

WE ALL FACE THE SAME NIGHTMARE, IF WE'RE LUCKY. ONE DAY they are mom and dad, our constants, our touchstones. The next, without warning, they are *old people.* They rely on us as we once leaned on them. No matter how much we love them, the inversion is fraught with ambivalence—for what it demands of us, and what it prefigures.

In 1988, at age fifty, I was working like a bandit as co-anchor for the top-rated local station. When my seventy-three-year-old father went into Good Samaritan Hospital that September, for the first of many bouts with pneumonia, I had no time to focus on anyone but me. I kept my assistant busy checking up on him, as I had with my mother's hysterectomy five months earlier. My caring was real, but mostly once removed.

Though my father recovered, his decline was plain. Once he got lost driving home from the grocery, taking an hour for a ten-minute trip. "I just took the wrong turn," he grumbled, after his wife dropped the dime on him. "Your mother was fussing so much that I lost track of where I was."

Never highly motivated, my dad surrendered. He blew

up to 220 pounds, aggravating the arthritis in his ankles
and feet. He was hard-put to negotiate the stairs to the
den, home to his TV set and cigarettes and Johnnie
Walker Red. My mother took to serving dinner down
there; he was good for but a single huffing trip a day.

As one who still pictured the sweet sprinter, the lean-
muscled athlete, I found it hard to watch my father atro-
phy. I nagged him about smoking and fried food, and the
benefits of exercise, and my urgings went in one ear and
out the other. When my mother thought I was too rough,
she might break in to say, "Poor Jackie, he's really tried,
you know." She had seen her man defeated long before
he lost his loping stride.

You could say that she'd given up, too.

Mama Tutt had been born with the century and was
sinking fast. Though cogent to the end, she'd stopped
eating. Nor could she stomach my father, even now, and
he took his revenge by refusing to drive out to the nursing home, her new address. My mother was forced to
take the Long Island Rail Road and then a subway to the
Bronx, a two-hour trip.

In November 1989, I joined her and Aunt Marian to
mark Mama Tutt's eighty-ninth birthday. When they
wheeled that stubborn, wonderful woman out in her
chair, she looked up at me sharply, as if to say, *Where
have you been?*

I said, "I'm sorry, Mama Tutt." It was too long since my
last visit. I tried to help feed her, but it wasn't any use. I
knew that we'd be losing her soon.

She died two weeks later.

With my station's new ownership wanting "a different
look," I was yanked off the anchor desk and sent back
into the field full-time. My mother and aunt, who considered me the best thing since Ed Sullivan, railed at the in-

justice. My father was more philosophical; he was used to disappointment.

As it turned out, my demotion was the best thing that could have happened to me. As senior correspondent, far from office politics, I could fly to any story I fancied and pass on any I did not, an unprecedented deal for a local station. Over the next five years, I would plunge into war zones and killing fields from Bosnia to the Middle East. My mother hated it when I ventured into harm's way. "Why does it always have to be you?" she said, after watching me dodge a few bullets in Somalia. "Why can't they send that old Bill Beutel for a change?"

They sent me because I was a danger junkie. I had a good nose in a tight spot; I'd tuned my radar on Gates Avenue. My treacherous childhood proved handy, time after time.

Besides, it was easier to deal with some obscure civil war than a crumbling marriage or a failing father. When my divorce from E. Jean became final, I took off for the Persian Gulf and Operation Desert Storm. After my passport was stolen in an altercation in Iraq, I escaped in a pitch-black drive to Saudi Arabia via Kuwait, just after the infamous turkey shoot. I passed scorched bodies and burning oilfields along a road dense with mines. But I felt comfortable in chaos, immune to the hazards around me.

Untouchable.

Untouched.

Three years earlier, Eric had married Sara Duffy, a model and native Minnesotan. On September 10, 1991, with my daughter-in-law in labor, I was having dinner downtown and checking in with my son by phone before each course. I never made it to dessert. With a midwife's assistance, Sara gave birth at home to a ten-pound boy. Twenty minutes later, I arrived in Brooklyn and leapt out of my car. At the top of my lungs I yelled up to their fourth-floor flat, "Patrick Emmanuel, this is your grand-father! Welcome to the world!"

Elated, I ran up the stairs and presented my gift to my son, an intricately carved African cane. He was the man now, the one who would pass it all down.

Through her sixties, even after she retired from the comptroller's office, my mother stayed vigorous. She never got sick, never sat still. Even as her hair grayed and her body thickened, I thought that she'd defy aging.

I was wrong, of course. All those hard years weighed down on her, stole her old darting energy. Noticeably heavy, she ran short of breath between bedroom and den. She grumped about her knees. She sounded like someone's great-grandmother, which she was.

There was the summer day when my mother insisted upon making a Brunswick stew. She asked me to reach for the spices, a telling concession. The stew itself, once a sure-fire hit, was overcooked and oversalted. Something was *off.*

A month or so later, I threw a seventy-third birthday lunch for my favorite twins at my rented house in Rock-land County. Today, thanks to video, I can remember my mother as she was—mischievous, darling, irrepressible. With gusto she told the story of her Mother's Day deba-cle, adding a chorus of "Jesus Loves Me" for old times' sake. "I was *ready* when that WABC van came for me," she exclaimed. "Johnny said, 'Mom, I'm not speaking to you anymore,' and I said, 'I don't care, because I will be getting lots of fan mail.' Which I did."

When I watch the tape, I see my father sitting limply in his deck chair beside her. He was a man of few words by then. I see my mother absently stroking his arm, or smoothing the fringe of white hair on the back of his head. She cared for him by reflex.

By the fall, my mother looked positively unwell. She was pale and bloated, given to sweats and chronic indigestion. Once or twice she fainted. She saw her doctor for tests, but they found nothing wrong.

In late October 1991, I flew to Madrid for the story of the hour, the first face-to-face peace talks between Israel and its Arab neighbors, including the PLO. Soon I was running on fumes. In addition to my three daily spots on WABC, I did live reports for network affiliates across the country. The work was grueling, competitive, charged—the journalism I loved best. I'd covered the Middle East before and knew the players on both sides. I was there because I could deliver the goods, on time and on the money.

Each day I called Ana Maria, my assistant in New York. After beginning as my intern at *Eyewitness News,* she'd become much more: my fix-it person at the studio, my right hand. Everything filtered through Ana Maria. When my kids needed to speak with me, they called her first. She'd become especially close to my mom, the daughter Irene never had.

"She doesn't sound right," Ana told me after I arrived in Madrid.

"What do you mean?"

"She just doesn't sound . . . *confident,* like she usually does."

Two days later, one of the network's brightest stars—a name familiar to any habitué of Nightly News Land—arrived on location with half a dozen producers in tow. As I wrapped a feed in front of the palace where the talks were being held, he complained about sharing equipment with a "local" correspondent. When informed that camera positions were at a premium, and that ABC had but one, the Big Gun pitched a fit.

Inside an hour, a second camera—an aging, portable field unit for quick remotes and stand-ups—was set on a tripod next to the studio model coveted by the Big Gun. This was where I would work henceforth. The critical difference: The second camera could not be cued with a TelePrompTer. As a result, my live reports would need to be memorized or ad-libbed, a dicey proposition when you're logging twenty-hour days and find yourself fumbling for the name of an anchor in Dallas or San Diego. The Big Gun, meanwhile, would read his brief script on tape before slipping off to a three-hour dinner at Madrid's finest restaurant.

He had won, but it wasn't enough for him to win. As I stood by later that day, my countdown sounding in my earpiece, the Big Gun barked out, "Don't you have something to do in Bedford-Stuyvesant?" It was a clear attempt to rattle me on the air, and it nearly worked.

By then I'd offended a second network luminary by scooping him on his turf. As he and the Big Gun walked off, he said, "Why don't you go back to your shoeshine stand?"

Through all the years that I'd covered kings and fools, presidents and pretenders, the bellwether stories of my time, I'd felt the weight of the race on my shoulders. I had to look great, sound great, *be* great for my mother and a million people like her. And no matter how many Emmys I won, or how many zeroes graced my paycheck, each day in the media reminded me that I was a black man. In Madrid the reminder was a poleax between the eyes— not so different, I suppose, than what my father must have felt at the colored emergency room in Washington, D.C.

I was still boiling as I got back to my hotel for a shower and a catnap. When I called home, Ana had the results from the last battery of tests. Her voice was strange, telegraphing the punch to come. The doctors, she said, had found an obstruction in my mother's colon.

I said, "Is it cancer?" The word rang strangely in my head, like syllables from a lost language.

Ana said, "They think so, but they can't be sure without surgery."

My mother's symptoms had led me to fear the worst. I was not shocked; I was merely destroyed. I dropped the phone on its cradle, and I cried and cried. I lost all sense of where I was.

The slights I'd suffered that day held no meaning. Everything would be different now. The boulder had been nudged from the top of the hill. It was rolling slowly for the moment, but soon it would be crashing along, turning trees to kindling and hurling birds to flight, until it was upon me. It had my name on it.

I'd pushed hard for success, and savored its trappings, but as a means to some nobler end. At first I'd tried to save the world. I lowered my sights after Attica, when I realized the world was beyond me, but still I thought I could save my parents. I could protect them from meanness, and make them proud, and keep them whole. Now I saw my dream of rescue for what it was: an empty fantasy. I could save no one, not even the one I loved best.

Nor could I escape. For so long I had used work and travel to run from my entanglements. But even a varsity runner cannot hide, not at the end, not when it matters. The clock had struck. It was time to pay for my peregrinations.

I was in a luxury hotel room in downtown Madrid, and my mother was dying.

I was glued to my ego-feeding job—master of the moment, confidant to those in high places—and my mother was dying.

An hour earlier I'd played the pluperfect correspondent, my Dolce & Gabbana tie trimly knotted, ready for whatever the anchor might ask. But now only one question mattered, the one I stood helpless to answer:

How can I live without her?

Back home, I rushed out to North Babylon. My heart sagged when I saw her, weaker than when I'd left, with new lines in her cheeks and forehead. As I propped on a smile and put the best face on things, my mother seemed worried most about my father. What would happen to him if she got really sick? I told her, "You've got to worry about *you* now, you know."

A week later, a CAT scan showed a blockage the size of a grapefruit. Surgery was set for November 20. With the help of my doctor and good friend, George Kessler, a geriatric specialist, I took a crash course on colon cancer. I submerged into a new and haunting vocabulary: *malignancy . . . metastasis . . . neoplasia . . .* When I told George what I knew of my mom's condition, he admitted that it didn't sound good.

I was irate. Why hadn't they caught the tumor earlier? Why hadn't I gotten her in to see George months before? I lobbied to move the surgery to Sloan-Kettering or Mount Sinai, where my fancy Manhattan friends went. Irene Johnson had settled for the second-rate at every turn, but no more. Now her life was at stake. Now she needed the best.

But my mother did not question authority lightly. She had faith in her family doctor: "He's good, and he knows me." The surgery had to be done at Good Samaritan, she explained, because it was a twenty-minute ride for Jackie. My counterpoint fell on deaf ears. She was placidly unmovable.

For years I had painted my father as the fossilized parent, resistant to any change. Now I realized that my mother was no less set in her ways. She sought my sympathy, not my guidance. She wanted to be heard, not to listen. At the end of the day, she was competent to make her own decisions, and who was I to know better? Everyone agreed that a cancer patient's attitude was crucial to survival. It could be dangerous to push my mother into hands she did not trust, regardless of credentials.

So I did what little I could. I checked on the surgeon through an oncologist friend, and got a positive report. I met him the day before my mother went in: a nice-looking, white-haired, Welby-esque fellow in his early sixties. His first task was to remove the obstruction, he said. If it was malignant, and he had to take too much of the colon, he might have to do a colostomy.

My heart sank. To live with a bag on her side would crush whatever healthy vanity my mother had left. When I saw her that evening, she already knew the score. I said, "It's going to be okay, Mom. You're going to come out of this." Yes, she said, her brave front in place. Yes, she was going to be fine.

I stayed with my father that night. He could hardly walk by then, and counted on neighbors for meals.

He said, "Mama's really sick, isn't she?"

I said, "Yes, she's very sick."

"Could she die?" Worry etched his face. I didn't want to scare him, but he had to change his ways. His wife would need support like never before.

I said, "It's a serious operation, Dad," and left it at that. I knew how scared he was, because I felt the same way.

The procedure lasted four and a half hours. When I spotted the surgeon heading my way, my heart began thumping. *Please God, don't let her die!*

"Your mother's doing well," he said, and that was the extent of his good news. They had found a raging cancer. "and I hope we got everything, but I can't be positive."

There was one more thing. The colostomy.

I felt a jumble of emotion: relief that my mother had survived, pain for what she'd endured, concern for the future. By the next day, her dismay cut through the narcotics. She said, "I've got to learn how to change the bag."

I said, "So what? They'll teach you how to do it. It's just great that you're alive." But we were both repelled by what had happened to her. It was a tough thing to swallow.

A week later she came home, with a nurse and Aunt Marian to help. The three of them barely fit into the narrow bathroom, which wasn't designed for an ailing woman and her immobile husband.

My mother did learn how to change her colostomy bag. It was time-consuming, though, and more than once I offered to help. Each time she turned me down. She never wanted me to see it, and secretly I was grateful.

In January 1992, two months after the surgery, my mother fought off fatigue to attend my daughter Christina's dance recital. Though her face was drawn and her step a bit halting, she felt blessed to be there.

The recital was the first of many events to be freighted with significance, now that our supply seemed finite. I saw my mother's will to live—and live fully—before she died, and my frustration fell into perspective. Yes, she might be limited in what she was willing to alter. But my mother placed second to no one in her capacity to *withstand.* To survive what life threw at her. To put one foot in front of the other, and go on.

My father was falling apart. My mother refused to ride with him anymore, calling a car service instead. She was out of harm's way when he backed his Ford down the driveway, overshot, and crashed into a parked car across the street.

When asked for an explanation, he stole from Fats Waller: "You know how big my feet are!"

"Yeah . . . ?" He wore a size 13, but I failed to see the relevance.

"Well, I had to pick up my knee and my knee hurt, and my foot came down on the wrong pedal."

"You mean you hit the accelerator instead of the brake?"

"That's right!" he said.

The old cabbie was skidding toward that Big Parkway in the Sky, and I had to tell him that his driving days were over. I confiscated his keys, a horrible thing to do to anyone, much less to the man who'd first put me behind a wheel. I thought about the time when I had lusted for my freedom and chafed at his restrictions. Now our roles had reversed, and I liked it no better.

Not long after that, my father fell down the stairs to the living room. While escaping with a bump on the head, he could not get up. My mother had to summon the neighbors to boost him to his feet and back to the bedroom.

My mother was fed up. Aside from the cooking and cleaning and laundry, she helped my father put on his pants. She tied his shoes. "He's lazier than ever," she said. "I can't keep on like this. I'm sick of it."

I'd been urging my parents for years to move into an assisted living center, or at least a house without stairs. As my dad's slide worsened, a nursing home seemed the only answer. I said, "Mom, you've got to think about Daddy. He's too much for you to take care of."

My father said, "Well then, you'll have to put me in some place." He was more than willing to go.

Changing her tack in mid-reproof, my mother said, "Yeah, I bet you'd like that. You'd have *more* people waiting on you hand and foot." For all her weariness, she was terrified of being left behind.

The discussion was tabled, but not for long. When I called one night from Miami, on location for a special on gun-running, my mother sounded shaky: "Your father's not well." He'd downed a shot of Scotch and he was gone—disoriented, unresponsive.

Even on a good day, my father seemed confused. His memory skipped like a scratchy LP. The cunning agitator had exited the stage, leaving a simpler man—grouchy and selfish, for sure, but essentially benign. When he asked the same question for the fourth time in an hour, my mother caught my eye and said, "Just like his mother."

In her old age, Grandmother Johnson was flooded by

dementia. When I was in my late teens and went with my father to her nursing home, she called me Jackie.

"No, Grandma, I'm Johnny."

She glanced at my father and said suspiciously, "Then who's that?"

"That's Daddy, that's your son."

My father said, "That's right, Ma. *I'm* Jackie!"

She shook her head; she wasn't buying it. I felt sorry for my father, who could never please the old lady and now had ceased to exist. But most of all I felt sad for Grandmother Johnson. I wanted to see her strutting in her fancy church dress, full of gumption and gossip, not sitting in a chair with her hair all wild and an amnesiac's frown on her face.

Thirty-five years later, the wheel had turned to the next generation. I looked into home care, but heard too many horror tales. We stumbled along for another month or so until events overtook us, as they often do.

In March 1992, I was neck deep in the first Clinton campaign when the candidate was still an underdog. I hopped down to Arkansas and rang up his mother, Virginia Kelley. She was real folks, a lot like my own mom, and we settled into her living room to watch Gennifer Flowers spill her story. My station cut to me for a live remote: "Here's what Bill Clinton's mother had to say about it!" (Virginia said that she'd never met Ms. Flowers, who wasn't a girl you brought home to mom, I suppose, especially if you were married.)

Back home, another siege of pneumonia had my father in and out of the hospital. A CAT scan confirmed several mini-strokes, which helped explain his mental lapses. He was no longer walking, and the hospital would not release him to his split-level house. Aunt Marian and I went to my mother in a united front. There was no alternative. He would have to go to a home.

Under Medicaid rules, my father could have been

placed anywhere within a fifty-mile radius. Pulling every string I could, I found him a bed in the East Neck Nursing and Rehabilitation Center, which had a spotless reputation and a mostly white clientele. I liked the facility's clean smell and its sun-soaked rooms. Best of all, it was a ten-minute cab ride from my parents' house.

Within days of my father's admittance, we saw a transformation. Once his medicines were governed and alcohol forbidden, he turned touchy and contentious, like his old self. As my mother had predicted, he was thrilled to command a professional staff. The only catch was the physical therapist, who hoped to get him walking again. My father avoided the man like the plague.

He was, in short, as happy as a clam—unless he ran out of cigarettes, when he'd put up a stink and refuse to leave his bed. To replenish his stockpile, I'd stop at a nearby pharmacy for three or four cartons of Carlton filters. "Boy," the counterman would say, "you sure do smoke a lot." They were rationed through the nurses, a pack a day, though my father would wheedle for more.

Shrewdly, he'd set aside a few smokes to bribe a spry old fellow named Steve, another black resident. Steve was the perfect flunky, physically hale but a little shaky upstairs. He did my father's bidding and ran his errands; essentially he replaced my mother, without the back talk. Steve wheeled his boss wherever he needed to go: the dining room, the bingo parlor, and—most important—the lounge, where my father chain-smoked by the television.

Soon the head nurse was calling me like a principal with a wayward eighth-grader. Mr. Johnson was smoking in his room, in his *bed*—a serious infraction, particularly when his roommate was on oxygen. When a nurse surprised him, he'd drop his lit cigarette into a bag that hung from the arm of his wheelchair. They cracked down on his match supply and confiscated several lighters, but he smuggled in more through Steve. He stayed one step ahead of the law. They couldn't lay a glove on him.

After seventy-six years, my father had found paradise.

By any objective measure, life was easier for my mother. She was free of her husband's demands and deadweight. She could baby herself now. She could live a little.

She hated every minute of it.

Since joining my father in retirement, my mother had spent most of her waking hours bossing him around. Without him, her life held no purpose. Her fastidious housekeeping began to slip. She took less care with her clothes. She was lost.

Her strength had dwindled since the surgery, but the malaise ran deeper than that. Why trouble to make things pretty? Why bother cooking for one? When my mother married, she'd moved straight from Mama Tutt to her husband. She hadn't spent a single night alone, and had no business starting now.

I made my pitch to Aunt Marian to sell her co-op in the Bronx, but she refused to live "in the country." I entreated my mother to return to the city, to join her sister and have some fun. But she wouldn't bend: "I can't be so far away from Daddy. Who's going to go see him if I'm out there?" Stalemate.

I came out to visit once or twice a week. I escorted my mother to meetings of the Birthday Club—a group that organized trips and cruises—and sat for hours, smiling and patient, with elderly people I did not know. Mostly I brought her to East Neck, where she visited each day. As we entered my father's room, she'd sniff the corrupted air and say, "I can tell you've been smoking in here, Jackie!"

My father would sigh loudly and reply, "Oh, Irene, just leave me alone." With that they'd be off to their fussbudget jamboree. My mother would catch my father leering at a nurse, or at a blue-haired siren flashing some varicose thigh. She'd say to me, "See, he hasn't changed. Nothing's changed!"

But everything had changed. Though she still made my father crazy a few hours a day, she no longer ruled his roost. He had his own life at East Neck, complete with checkers partners and valet. I would say that she missed him more than he missed her. If she was smothering in loneliness, he had found some welcome breathing space.

"Oh, your father's doing *fine,*" she'd tell me, her anger transparent. In a marriage riddled with indignities, that might have been the cruelest of all.

I spent that summer working eighteen-hour days on the campaign trail. When out of town, I orchestrated my parents' lives long-distance. When back in New York, I took over their affairs: bills, taxes, health insurance, home maintenance. It was my turn now. I made sure everything was paid on time; I wanted to reflect well on them.

I called my mother each morning to check that she had cab fare to the nursing home. I'd touch base again midday on the line I had installed in my father's room. My dad and I might have a brief chat (*Don't forget my cigarettes, boy!*), but the phone belonged mostly to my mother.

I called a third time at night, after the late news. My mother still analyzed each show, but she couldn't veil the sadness in her voice. She sounded wan, deflated. Unlike Aunt Marian, who'd become a rabid Mets fan, my mother had few outside interests. My father was her hobby, her job, her nuisance, her companion—the bane of her existence and the love of her life. Now that they slept apart, TV sitcoms filled the void. The house was too quiet, the memories too strong.

I would imagine her lying in the set's bluish glow, huddled to the edge of a half-empty bed. I worried that she might turn to her old, beckoning friend, to the man in the cork hat, in drunks' lingo. But my mother insisted there was nothing for me to worry about. She belonged to a dogged generation. She did not like to complain.

Before hanging up, she would say, "You just take care of yourself."

After our good nights, I'd dial my assistant and my daughter-in-law to follow up on this or that the next day. The smallest detail would not evade me, yet I knew that I should be doing more.

The twins' seventy-fourth birthday party that August was a festive occasion. But my smile faded whenever I peeked at my mother, in her glory as the doting matriarch. She looked puffy, as when she'd first fallen ill. Though the last round of tests showed no recurrence of the cancer, I knew that our time was on loan. Would it be our last reunion? My mother's last birthday?

Two days earlier, I'd traded in my Mercedes and my vintage Corvette for a used red Ferrari. I wasn't out to buy a status symbol; I simply craved a real-life sports car, the fastest crate available without booster rockets. I needed to do something irresponsible. I'd be damned if I'd be wistful at seventy, and life was getting shorter all the time.

As Ferraris work better when driven hard, I took my new toy to some race car folks to add a wee more speed. After a few skillful tweaks (and the removal of the catalytic converter), my round-trips to East Neck became the best part of my day. My favorite times were late at night, streaking home through light traffic. With the coupé's top detached, I would red-line through the gears, carving through the air like Mario Andretti.

I discarded the radar detector, since the point of a Ferrari is to tempt fate. I got ticketed on the Palisades Parkway for whizzing into triple digits, and was obliged to attend a driver safety class, but I wanted *more* speed. The scarier the ride, the greater the thrill—and the more road between me and the dying. During one desolate midnight ramble on the Long Island Expressway, when the panel claimed an unlikely 147 miles per hour, it felt almost like flight.

When someone you love is in trouble, each day is a rotation on Jupiter, an endurance test. Yet the weeks do pass and the world spins on, careless of your troubles. Each minute is precious, but it expires nonetheless. You relax your guard. You adapt to the status quo, ominous as it may be.

For a year my parents stayed reasonably healthy. In that interim I moved to a serene mountain tree house in a more remote part of Rockland County. My new address was miles from the nearest store, and you'd need a four-wheel drive to get up to me in the winter. If I was seeking a hermit's haven, I had found one.

I was unpacking when my son Eric called. "Grandma's sick," he said, sounding alarmed. I tore out to the Island, where I found my mother in her nightgown. She was disheveled, incoherent, quite out of her head.

Aunt Marian arrived, gave her sister a hug, and said sharply, "What's wrong with you, Irene?"

"I'm all right," my mother said. "I'm all right . . . I'm all right." She sank into her chair, staring into the middle distance. I wondered if she'd had a stroke, or gotten into the rum.

When they found no alcohol in her bloodstream, the doctors guessed at a drug imbalance. I wished it were that simple. My mother had sent us a subliminal message. She was lonely and depressed, and she didn't want to be in that house anymore. She wanted to be with my father.

And though I would not say it in so many words, I wanted anything but. In his sloth and indifference, my father was East Neck's happiest camper. But my mother was too active to enter a nursing home, too able and independent. I hated the thought of her caving in.

At the same time, I knew that she had few options. She'd spent the last half-century bound to one man, and she had to play her hand out to the end. It was way too late to ask for a new deal.

In April 1993, I was half a world away in Egypt, shooting a series on Islam in the wake of the World Trade Center bombing. Upon arriving I played Lawrence of Arabia, riding horseback to the pyramids. The next day we drove south of Cairo to the dusty hometown of Ramzi Yousef, who was later convicted of masterminding the attack. After we interviewed his relatives, the authorities arrested us and took our footage. (Fortunately, they confiscated the wrong tape.)

In the midst of this excitement, I received sobering news from Ana Maria: My mother had relapsed. A blockage in her small intestine, scar tissue from the surgery, had set off a massive infection. Running a high fever, restricted to a liquid diet, she was alternately ravenous and nauseated.

Cutting my trip short, I rushed home via London and spent the next several days between Good Samaritan and WABC, where my series entered postproduction. At one point I fell asleep in my office chair. I prided myself on writing my own material, but this time I couldn't finish, nor was I able to shoot all I'd planned. The Islam series would be adequate, but less than what it might have been.

In the office, my brain was AWOL. I could not break loose from the gray miasma around my head, the dull pressure in my chest. I knew that my mother was resting on quicksand. She was sinking away from me, a little further each day.

In my heart, I felt I should be with her all the time.

A week after my return, my mother slipped into delirium. Her liver was barely working. She couldn't keep anything down, a chilling reminder of Mama Tutt's last days. The doctors had to go in to remove the scar tissue, but their hands were tied by the infection. They moved her into a single room in intensive care—into the place, I was certain, for people bound to die.

On Saturday, April 24, I kept a lecture date at a synagogue and asked the congregation to add my mother to their prayers. On Sunday she was semiconscious and in horrific pain, writhing from one side of the bed to the other. Each breath was a heaving grunt, each word a killing labor. She asked me to rub her legs, and I did, but she needed help beyond any I could provide. The line had broken. The enemy was at the gate.

For a time she fell silent. Then her eyes fluttered open and she whispered, "I'm going to go." I sat close by the bed, holding her papery hand. Her eyes rested on Ana Maria and she said, "Promise to take care of Johnny for me."

I took my mother into my arms and told her that she could not go. I held her tight and begged her to stay. I coached her as hard as I'd coached Patsy in birthing our first daughter, with the same laser focus, except now I was coaching against death.

Mama, Mama, please Mama, don't be dying Mama, you're not gonna die!

It wasn't enough. I could feel my mother leaving. She breathed out from the deepest part of her being, deeper than the body that housed her. It went on forever as I lay against her, a stake against an ill wind.

Seconds—eons—dragged by before I felt my mother's diaphragm shuddering to inhale, her lungs rallying from that deep, deep place. I will tell you this: I willed my mother back to life. She came back. She was dying, and she came back. Within twenty-four hours her fever abated. The immediate crisis passed.

On Monday I faced a grim choice. Without surgery, there was no hope. My mother might never eat solid food again. Her future would be measured in weeks, if not days.

On the other hand, the procedure was highly risky, even with her fever down. If my mother came through it, her life would be extended. But the odds of her surviving were no better than even.

There was little to lose, yet I agonized. Given my mother's condition, the decision was properly mine. But it was a terrible weight to hold my mother's life in my hands. I had to take on more adulthood when I felt most like a child. I wished I had a sibling to share the load.

"That's fine," she said, when I told her what I thought. My mother had utter trust in her son. Once I endorsed a course of action, the discussion was closed.

The next morning I sat alone on a hard chair in Good Samaritan's waiting room. Its cool bareness evoked a confessional. I'd thought it apt to keep my vigil to myself, but now I wasn't so sure. The wait was torture. What if she died? How could I live with myself?

And again: *How could I live without her?*

Aside from weddings and funerals, I had not set foot in a church for twenty years. Like Pascal, however, I hedged my bets. I beseeched God for the mercy that my mother deserved. I pleaded for her life. I prayed with my eyes clenched, my stomach knotted, my head swimming.

I was still praying when the nurse came out to tell me the surgery was over, and my mother was fine.

CHAPTER TWELVE

OUR NEAR-DEATH EXPERIENCE BROUGHT ALL TO A HEAD. THOUGH my mother convalesced in good shape, it made no sense to send her home. She'd been worn down by dealing with my dad all day, then coping with a barren house at night. She wasn't safe living alone. What if she fell down the stairs?

I wasn't prepared to make radical changes to meet my mother's needs. (*Quit my job? Move out to Long Island?*) Which left us with the nursing home. While my mother technically didn't belong there, she needed to be with her husband and could not care for him herself. Her social worker grasped the situation, as did the people at East Neck: They were kind enough to stretch their criteria and accept her.

Still, I wrestled with the decision. At fifty-four, I had seen my children through college, and retirement was not so far away. My load would be lightened if my parents were together in the home. But was I taking the easy path, the self-serving path? I'd grown up in a tight-knit extended family. Mama Tutt lived with Aunt Marian until the end of her life; Grandma Johnson lived next to Uncle

Manzie for much of hers. I had more to give than those before me, and yet I was giving less.

My mother had sown what she'd reaped. From nearly the instant of my conception, she'd devoted her entire being to my success. She'd done such a good job that my life had grown too large for me to cede in return.

After a number of restless nights, I finally approached her: "Mom, I think it would be good if you were in the home with Dad. How do you feel about that?"

"I wouldn't mind," she said, and her smile spoke volumes.

My parents' friends and neighbors would disparage me for moving my mother to East Neck. But none of them saw the grin that split her face the day she was admitted. Her labors were done. Her worries lay forgotten. When I rolled her down the corridor, she waved like the Rose Bowl queen. She already knew the cast—the patients, the visitors, the doctors and nurses and staff. Now she was a full member of their society. Now she belonged.

Look, it's Irene—and her son!

Hi, Irene!

How you doing, Irene? Welcome home!

As we made our deliberate way, my mother sat straighter in her chair. Something switched back on. She wasn't some ailing, failing old woman—she was *Irene* again. Rather than lose herself inside an institution, she'd regain her identity there.

By the time we entered 312, the room she'd be sharing with my father, she was positively shining. I had moved all my parents' furniture that could fit: the big armoire, the dresser, the two recliners. Plus their stereo and two large televisions, so my father could follow his sports while my mother watched *60 Minutes*. Plants and photographs crowded the surfaces; my father's caps dotted the wall. The room was cozy, familiar, reassuring.

Most important, they were together. Reunited with her Jackie, my mother knew all would be well. East Neck was a long stretch from Gates Avenue, a very different kind of ghetto. In a circuitous way, however, she'd come home. She looked at me and said, "This is the best thing in the world for me."

My father was less elated. "Oh, Lord, here she comes," he muttered, as I lugged the bags through the door. No more in-room smoking when my mother was there to police it, no more pinching of nurses without hell to pay.

The party was over. The sheriff was back in town, to stay.

It is bizarre to be on television and come into people's homes each night. If you last enough years on the small screen, you acquire an extended Nielsen family. People root for you as though you were one of their own.

My celebrity paid off big-time for my parents. It smoothed their entry into a top nursing home, won them attention above-and-beyond. Even when I was gone for weeks at a time, in Israel or South Africa, I remained a presence on the tube: East Neck's favorite son.

My mother was easy to serve. She took a motherly interest in her caregivers, and tipped them well for getting her toothpaste or nail polish remover, or an occasional takeout meal. I made sure that she had a few hundred dollars in her purse, so she'd never be caught short.

My father, that crotchety guy with the wandering hands, was another story. Yet even he got special treatment at East Neck, especially from the middle-aged black women to whom I was a local hero. Room 312 was invariably spic and span, its residents the same. My parents were treated like guests at a resort that happened to house a crack medical staff. From morning to night, a parade of workers ducked in to be of service.

*Do you need anything now, Mrs. Johnson? New
Kleenex? Want me to run out for something?*

*Does Mr. Johnson need anything? Should we turn
him over?*

*I saw John on the news today—can I get some of
that lotion you like, come back and rub your feet later?*

Soon my mother regained her old vigor. She wrote for
the in-house newsletter and joined a resident council.
("Irene was very vocal," her social worker logged, "about
having compassion and trying to calm noisy/disruptive
residents by speaking to them directly in a nice cheerful
voice.") As she got stronger, she joined the bus trips to
the beach or Belmont Park Racetrack. Whenever I could,
I'd come along.

Other times we'd have our own outings. My mother's
favorite spot was the Landmark Grill, an Italian restaurant
where the proprietor bowed and scraped: *Oh, Mrs. Johnson, it is so good to see you again* . . . She loved the red-
carpet treatment nearly as much as the fried shrimp and
three white wine spritzers, which she sipped through
dinner. Though she'd developed cirrhosis, on top of her
other problems, I wouldn't deny her the occasional treat.
She'd get back to the home half-loaded and happy.

If anything, my mother enjoyed a busier social life
than before. At Thanksgiving and again at Christmas, I
arranged for catered dinners in the game room. There
were visits from the Birthday Club, including some of my
erstwhile critics. As they began to age dramatically themselves, and saw my mother so carefree, their disapproval
turned to envy.

Aunt Marian was less impressed. It galled her to see
her sister in a nursing home with that good-for-nothing
husband. Here was the crowning proof that Black Jack
had dragged poor Fatty down.

As usual, Fatty turned a deaf ear. For my mother, all that
counted was to take her meals with my father in the din-

ing room, at a rear corner table reserved just for them. Or to listen to him sleeping and whisper to the nurse the next morning, "I think I heard Jackie wheezing last night."

True, she took her husband to task for the cigarette burns on his shirts and his filthy habits in general. Unbowed, he'd sneak a quick smoke when she was down the hall or in the bathroom. My mother combed his drawers and dug under his pillow for contraband: "Jackie, you're going to set this place on fire. I'm not going to die in here from your damn smoking!" They snipped at each other in fine form. They'd simply moved their act on the road.

My mother wouldn't have had it any other way.

On January 6, 1994, Virginia Kelley died. I remembered her warmth the day we met in Arkansas, and how she'd sought me out for a hug at the convention after her son clinched the nomination. I thought about how sad Bill Clinton must be; I wasn't likening myself to a president, but I sensed that he was a mama's boy like me. I was more conscious these days of what it meant to lose a mother, having come so close myself.

Two weeks later, with the help of my Realtor friend, Marcy Lawrence, I sold the house in North Babylon. Against my advice, my parents had willed the property to each other, thereby funneling the proceeds to the nursing home for reimbursement. After all their hard work, they would leave nothing tangible behind.

Telling the neighbors to take whatever furniture was left, I skipped the closing and never went back. I remembered how my parents had struggled to buy that house, how much it had meant to leave their ratty apartment—and how young they were then, in their prime. It was something for them to live under their own roof, on their small plot of land.

We'd had good times in North Babylon and some bad ones, too. But now it was over and my parents were old, and their house but a faceless pile of bricks.

That March, when my father was hospitalized with a respiratory flare-up, my mother worried every waking minute. *If your father coughs, your mother gets pneumonia . . .* I'd viewed her love for him as an act of self-denial, but now I saw it was something more. She *needed* to keep him up and running and content. She could not conceive of a life without him.

To cheer her up, I stopped at Macy's and grabbed a dress off the rack, taking little trouble or expense. I suppose I was thinking, *Where is she going to wear this, anyway?*

When my mother opened the box and her face fell, I wanted to sink through the floor. The dress looked dowdy and didn't fit her right. It was as though I'd written her off as an attractive woman.

Too late, I saw that everything had to be more special now, not less. Pressing my apologies, I scooped up the stupid rag and put it back in the box.

The next day I went to Bloomingdale's and spent a small fortune on a dress that was worthy of the woman who would wear it.

For nearly a year I'd been working on a trip to Cuba. After meeting Castro's emissaries in Miami, New York, and Washington, I gradually gained their trust. I was promised full access to Havana and the countryside. An interview with Fidel—a feat for any correspondent—was in the bag.

On June 13, 1994, the day before I was set to leave, the O. J. Simpson story broke. Given my seniority, I had an ironclad excuse not to follow the pack to California. But while Cuba was the better story, O.J. was bigger, much bigger. My journalist's soul murmured *Havana*; my tabloid ego said I'd be a sucker to miss the murder trial of the century. My mom and dad, in stable shape of late, didn't need so much attention. I had no good reason not to enlist.

Just like that, Fidel was history.

My parents were thrilled by my plum assignment. They were convinced that O.J. was being framed and that only Johnny Boy could save the day. My mother said, "He didn't do it, but there's a bunch of racists who want to believe he did. You go out there and find the truth."

So I went. That summer I shuttled to Los Angeles for a variety of pretrial hearings and motions and news conferences. I could tell you that I didn't foresee the Simpson story swallowing my life. That's what I'd tell myself later, that I'd bitten off more than I anticipated.

But it wasn't an accident that I put three thousand miles between me and my parents. I found East Neck routinely heartbreaking; I hated finding out who'd disappeared last week. I dreaded my mealtime stroll through the ranks of the dying, to the corner table where a frail little couple sat eating their bland little lunch.

It rocked me every time: *They were dying, too.* My parents were winding down a one-way street, and nothing I could do would stop them. Were I a wealthier man, I might have booked a more deluxe facility. Their room might have overlooked a lake. But the plot line would be the same: the slowing rhythm; the tearful denouement; the inevitable ending, one size fits all.

What an evil life! I'd look at my father and confront the ghost of my future. Was this where I was headed, to be a guy like that in a place like this? I thought I would kill myself first—

"John?"

"Yes, Mom?"

"I want you to meet Mrs. Thompson, she watches you all the time . . ."

It was most intense at dinner. The big TV at the front of the room would be tuned to WABC, where I'd often be delivering some special taped report. I'd tread through a bog of well-wishers, leading up to my mother's thousand-watt smile.

I knew how to behave with people. I'd be gracious when introduced, reliably cheerful through my visits. My parents needed uplift, not neurosis. But the role began to enervate the actor. It points to a lack of courage, some constitutional defect, but I cannot deny it. Those visits ground me into the floor.

For a man on the run, the Simpson trial was made to order. In L.A. I was marooned on a far archipelago, immersed in the task at hand. There were no slow news days on the O.J. beat. Even weekends, when court was in recess, would be ripe with breaking developments. I was on television more often than Regis Philbin, hitting every news show live from noon to eleven. I stayed in the jury's hotel and cultivated prime sources. Attorneys favored me with sound bites. My adrenaline ran off the charts.

My mother would sooner miss a meal than a broadcast, and I called her after each one, as per tradition. She offered her standard raves, then passed the phone excitedly to my father: *Here, Jackie, say something to your son . . . Hi, Johnny, I liked that. That was good!*

It took me a while to register how relieved I felt in Los Angeles. As the weeks became months without a trip home, I spun comforting rationales. My parents were getting a huge kick out of my work. They were living through me, if not with me. And wasn't I visiting four times daily, through the miracle of the cathode ray tube?

I tried not to dwell on all I could not do, like holding someone's hand when she was hurting, or taking her to that cute Italian restaurant. My mother soldiered on, never allowing that she missed me. If I voiced my mis-givings, she'd say, "Oh, come on. It's okay, Johnny." I was on an important story; I was doing God's work.

As my mother's life whittled down, she became more purely selfless than ever. Her husband and son came first. As long as they were happy, all was well.

Back home for the holidays, I was struck by how much weight she had lost. Her face was gaunt and creviced; flesh hung loosely from her arms. When she stood to em-brace me, she seemed shaky on her feet. The relics of her old self—the lilting voice, the twinkling humor—itali-cized her descent. Here was what I'd been avoiding: the sight of a woman in the gun lap of her race.

We shared a light Christmas lunch at East Neck with my father, and then I took her to Ana Maria's family in New Jersey for dinner. Though my mother wasn't feeling well, she was poignantly happy to join the party. It was a good day.

We stayed the night at my new house, which she'd been eager to see. She took the main-floor bedroom while I camped upstairs, dozing fitfully, like a parent with a newborn. Each time she got up or so much as turned over, I'd scurry down to check on her.

We cut breakfast short; my mother needed to go home. The return trip fatigued her, and she was glad to pull into the familiar drive. She felt safe at East Neck, where she knew her way around and could use the bath-room without being self-conscious.

Her traveling days were done, I thought, her wander-lust a thing of the past. Years after I went off on my own, my parents had finally discovered Cape Cod and Niagara Falls. As my father wouldn't fly, I paid my mother's way to Mexico with Aunt Marian and to Hawaii with the Birthday Club. But she never made it to the land of *The Red Shoes,* to the bistros and museums I'd crowed about.

France became a metaphor for all that she'd missed in life.

Why hadn't I taken her to Paris, as I'd promised a dozen times? Was I too busy, or did something hold me back? I found comfort in my mother's company, but she also overwhelmed me. I was her light, her shining all. Our tie was so intense that it drained me to be with her one-on-one.

My mother was not blind to the ripples of her passing. I believe she went to Christmas dinner because she knew I was close to Ana Maria and her parents, and that I'd soon need a surrogate family. She was handing me on.

On New Year's Eve I called her from home a few minutes before midnight. As the ball dropped in Times Square, our defenses were down. We bared our deepest truths, as people do when the blade poises over their necks. I told her how much I loved her, and she said that she knew. I thanked her for being a wonderful mother; she deflected the praise.

"You've been such a good boy, Johnny," she said. "Such a good boy."

With the holidays concluded, I could have cited our emergency and begged off the O.J. beat. Instead I returned to Los Angeles. I could not stop my mother from dying, but I could sure as hell get out of the way.

As she got weaker, she turned inward. As her health flagged, it became the one topic worth discussing. The cancer was back on its rampage. There was leakage around the colostomy, prompting a new round of radiation.

On February 23, 1995, as Johnnie Cochran cross-examined Detective Tom Lange, and Christopher Darden lost his cool with Judge Ito, my mother was stricken with pain and rushed to Good Samaritan. When I phoned the hospital, the news was bad. They'd found spots on her lungs, and further therapy was pointless. The doctors could only broker the terms of surrender.

The strain caught up to me. I normally fed off the challenge of scooping the networks, but my heart elsewhere.

I told my boss to relieve me. On March 1, I took the red-eye home.

After fifteen days in the hospital, my mother was readmitted to East Neck. She could no longer walk. One afternoon, with my father out smoking, I found her in her wheelchair by the window, staring out at the lush woods. I paused in the doorway before saying hello.

My mother turned her head, surprised, then greeted me warmly. But it took her a second to rearrange her face, and in that lag I saw a tragic sadness. She had let down her guard and her demon had found her. It was not about her dying. It was something much worse.

"He doesn't love me," my mother said, more in wonderment than complaint. "I gave my all to that man, and he doesn't love me!"

After fifty-eight years, she'd taken inventory of her marriage and the sums fell short. As far as I could glean, there had been no kindling incident, no fresh outrage on my father's part. My mother had simply seen him with new eyes, like the time she stepped back from Tchelitchev's baby heads. Now the picture couldn't be sharper: She had given her love to a squandering man.

I'd never seen my mother so dejected. It was easy to read the glum questions in her head. Had she been a fool in loving him, as Mama Tutt had long insisted? Had she wasted her life?

I had to say something. I had to tell her that her life had meaning, that she'd done the right thing. So I said, "Yes he does, Mom. Daddy loves you. He just doesn't know how to show it." Amazingly enough, I halfway believed it.

As I left her that day, I realized how needy she'd been for my reassurances. I'd come back just in time. How could I have waited so long?

Over the next four weeks I tried to make up for six months of neglect. I saw my mother daily, pushed her to the cafeteria for a few small bites, sat by her bed for hours while she slept. I willed myself to stay positive, to suppress my self-pity. I am transparent around the people I care about; I could easily have dropped to the floor eight times a day. (*Please don't hurt! Please don't have cancer! Please don't die!*) But the times called for care and modulation. I could not let her sense there was no hope.

Inside my cool shell, however, I was undone. Death was buzzing in the background, a little louder each day, like white noise gone mad. It was filling Room 312 as I muffled my ears, and I could not keep it out.

In my other life, that shallow existence outside East Neck, I became impetuous, if not downright irrational. I traded up for an even faster Ferrari, a black Mondial. I gave an interview to E. Jean for a piece about the former men in her life, and was properly excoriated in *Esquire* as a lovesick, arrogant ninny.

In those days of earthquake, everything teetered, including my twenty-three-year association with *Eyewitness News.* In the wake of my work on the Simpson trial, rival WCBS offered me their lead anchor job, a long leap into the unknown. I was tenured at WABC, a part of the furniture; I had a sure thing to retirement. But anchoring would keep me closer to New York. Thanks to a non-compete clause in my current contract, I'd also get a three-month hiatus. I could be with my mother without distraction.

Not least, there was the lure of the top spot at a flag-ship station. I would be capping my career in style.

My mother had her good days and bad. On the morning the story broke, she was too weak to sit up. I raised her head as I read aloud the headline in the *Daily News*: "Anchor Away: John Johnson Jumping from Channel 7 to Channel 2." She smiled, the skin taut across her face, and said, "That'll show 'em!" She had never forgiven WABC for demoting me twelve years earlier. Where her boy was concerned, my mother could hold a grudge.

The next week she rallied. She asked me to invite the family out to see her "and make sure that Marian comes." I downplayed the event by asking if I should come, too.

She said, "Of course I want you to come." Once again I'd singed her feelings.

On March 26 I collected our small assembly: my cousin Dianne, and her husband; Aunt Marian; Ana Maria. My mother was waiting in the lobby as we entered, spruced up in her favorite blue dress. She looked so lovely and well that I nearly walked past her.

She had dressed for her farewell appearance.

We went up to her room and filled it with laughter. After the others left, I stayed on to talk. My mother took to musing about her sister: "Marian is such a good person—I love her so much." She went on, "Your Mama Tutt had such a hard time, it makes me sad to think about it. I don't know why your father didn't like her, but you know how your father was. He was jealous of everybody."

My mother frowned, but only for a moment. She searched my eyes, and a lump formed in my throat. She said, "You know, Johnny, you've given me everything good in my life. You made everything better for us. You've been a good son; you've been a good man. But you can't be alone, and I don't know if you'll ever be happy."

I could tell she was tiring. When I made to leave, she held my arm for one last piece of business. She said,

"Your father's just a poor soul, and he's done the best he could. You be sure you take care of him."

I said, "Of course I'll take care of him, but what are you talking about? I'll take care of both of you."

"No, Johnny, I mean it. Don't let him smoke in the room, now."

"Okay, I won't let him smoke in the room."

"And don't let him have any matches."

"Okay, Mom." I headed for the door before she could see my tears.

"But Johnny, one more thing?"

I looked back from the doorway: "Yes?"

"Make sure that he has his cigarettes."

My mother was a wise woman. She understood the father's need and the son's estrangement. It was as close as she'd come to a dying wish.

Over the next days she began slurring her speech. They moved her bed closer to my father's, to allow him to hold her hand. When the staff met with me to explain how ill she was, I indignantly cut them off—*Hey, you think I don't know this? Come on!*

I knew that my mother would eventually be dying, but I thought I could stave off the end. I could bring her back as I had two years before. She was seventy-six, a number that now seemed obscenely young. Even as her body shut down, I could not believe she was going. My evasions distanced me all around.

By March 30, my mother could no longer speak. The doctors told me that she would not last the fortnight. The next day I bowed to contingency and made funeral arrangements. The day after that, she fell into a semi-coma.

April 2 was a Sunday, my mother's favorite day of the week: church day, rest day. It would not be long, the doctors said. By mid-morning we had gathered in her room:

my father, my children, Ana Maria. Plus Adrienne, who'd treated my mother like her own.

Aunt Marian declined to join us. She knew that the patient was helpless, bound by tubes and apparatus, and she didn't want to see Fatty like that.

I sat to the left of the bed and held my mother's hand. I hung on each break between her breaths, praying it would not be the last. With her pain annulled by morphine, I willed her to hang on, and hang on. In the absence of a miracle, I was willing to play death to a draw.

It seemed that time had stopped. At one point I glanced behind me and noticed that my father was gone; Steve had wheeled him out for a smoke. My daughter-in-law went to take my restive grandson home. Leaning over the bed to plant a kiss, she let out a yelp. My mother's whole body was quaking.

"Mom?"

Her head and shoulders convulsed up off the bed; her eyes were open and rolling. I grabbed her with both arms. I heard that rattling sound that I knew too well, that last deep exhalation until nothing could be left, and I held my mother tight and implored her not to die—

"I-*rene!*" my father moaned, fresh from his cigarette break. "What are you doing, Irene? You can't leave me, I'm all alone! Who's going to take care of me now, Irene? Who's going to take care of me now?"

Not even in death, I thought, as she gasped her last in my arms. *He couldn't give her any peace, not even in death.* If my mother was at all conscious in her final moments on earth, my father's lamentation was the last thing she heard. How I hated him then! I could have gladly dragged him from his wheelchair and flung him from the room.

Instead I got up sobbing with the rest and numbly shuffled to the door while the nurses took over. As they closed the curtain, for some reason I peeked back, a bad idea. I had been *with* my mother in her dying, as close as you can get to someone in another skin. But her death was final and frozen. It had nothing to do with me. As the orderlies set about placing the body in a bag, she lay with her head cocked at an odd angle, her startled eyes fixed on mine. I stood frozen and horrified in turn.

That was my last image of my mother, the one burnt into memory. I saw a woman who'd lived in apprehension and loneliness, and who appeared to go out the same way.

CHAPTER THIRTEEN

I WATCHED IN ASTONISHMENT AS THEY KEPT FILING INTO THE BOYD Spencer Funeral Home in Babylon. Though I'd exhausted my mother's address books, I wasn't prepared for the response: a standing-room crowd of more than two hundred people. Nursing home staff, old city co-workers, suburban neighbors, elderly friends who could scarcely walk—they all turned out. Some drove ninety minutes or more to get there.

The funeral was remarkably integrated, a tribute to how Irene Johnson lived her life. A field of roses and daffodils layered the chapel. A photograph adorned the closed casket. My mother's smile reached the last row.

The scene was flawless, indisputably moving, but not for me. I'd been on autopilot for three days, doing what needed doing from a distant orb.

Out of respect to my mother's faith, I'd asked a priest to preside. He was a stranger to the deceased, though, and the eulogy fell to me. I had to do justice to my mother's buoyant spirit, to her goodness but also her mirth. I wrote nothing out; I knew I'd have no trouble finding words.

"Judging from everyone who's here, my mother was obviously some kind of special person," I began. "She'd be

having a great time, because she would never turn down
a party. She loved to dance and do her Shuffle Off to Buffalo. That's when you knew she'd had a little taste of her
Jack Daniel's."

My audience laughed and relaxed, and I told my
mother's story. I spoke of her hardscrabble youth, how
she'd come up North to be left destitute in Harlem. How
a strong black woman from Augusta, Georgia, my Mama
Tutt, raised those two fine little girls. I said, "It's an unbe-
lievable story. How could my grandmother do that? How
could they endure? But they found a way."

I remembered when I was small and lived for days on
Spam—"and sometimes we couldn't even afford Spam,
so we made do with surplus army rations. My mother
never forgot what it was to be poor and hungry. Maybe
that's why she was the most generous person I've ever
known. She wouldn't just give you a meal, she'd give you
the platter of leftovers to take home with you.

"When times got a little better, there was enough food
in our house to see us through a nuclear war. I could
bring a dozen friends over from City College—any time,
day or night—and my mother would go into her refrig-
erator and throw together her famous Brunswick stew.
Those white kids loved to come to my house in Bed-Stuy,
because my mother could *cook*."

While she didn't have much in material things, I went
on, my mother was an accomplished person, a voracious
reader and a gifted athlete. I told the story of how she
sprinted home for my father's keys before his bus left.
And how, without a day of college, she rose to supervisor
at every place she worked.

I looked at my dad in the front row, and I said, "My father had a great gift. He had my mother." I thanked her for
loving him so, and for her dedication to her son: "She
kept a little diary of the things that I did, and all of my report cards and certificates, and every article ever written

about me. She was a tough taskmaster, but she truly cared. Without her molding, I don't know where I would be today."

At that point it got difficult, but I had to see this through. I thanked each of her relatives and close friends by name for enriching her life. I especially thanked Sistah, my Aunt Marian, for being just that: a loyal and loving sibling.

I said, "I have lost my teacher, my biggest fan, and my best friend in one fell swoop. I loved my mother, and I will miss her forever. Forever. *Forever.* And my life will never be the same."

I talked for half an hour. When I finished, and they played "My Man's Gone Now," my mother's sorrowful favorite from *Porgy and Bess,* I was amazed that I did not cry. I held myself together like a veteran correspondent. Or like a boy who'd curbed his hurt at the most harrowing times.

I thought I was in the clear. I was fine through the burial, where a hundred people set roses on my mother's casket. The mourners dispersed in silence. The air felt oppressively still. It happened as I walked from the grave site to the limousine—my legs gave. I was disabled; I had to be physically helped into the car. As the door closed behind me, I lurched forward to my knees on the limo's plush floor, sobbing helplessly, holding on to my two sons for dear life. As we pulled away, and I saw that the casket had yet to be lowered, I kept asking Eric, "Is it all right to leave her here?" I felt like a deserter.

After lunch with the family, I returned my father to the nursing home. He'd carried himself beautifully through the services, debonair in his beret and neatly trimmed Vandyke. (My friends were incredulous that he was nearly eighty.) He'd been fussed over by people he hadn't seen in years. He had gotten his due.

Now there were the two of us, mano-a-mano, alone in a room with a stripped, empty bed. I had already passed my mother's clothing and recliner to the staff. *She filled that room,* one of her nurses would remember. But three days after her death, save for her pictures on the walls, she left no visible trace.

I had seen my share of dying and then some. I'd witnessed massacres and biblical famines; I once held in my palm a Somalian toddler weighing no more than a housecat. In the thick of the worst carnage, I was able to do my remote, a word that fit me perfectly. I didn't try to make sense of the universe. I didn't ponder the imponderables. I just got through the day.

But now that death had brushed my cheek, I was forced to take its measure. I found my mother's absence very strange. How could a person be with you one day and forever gone the next? How could we plan a future when the void hung over us, one failed breath away?

Breaking into my morbid reverie, my father said, "Are they going to put someone else in the room?"

"After a little while," I said. "It's a good thing. You should have company in here."

And then he said, "Are you going to come to see me?"

"Of course I'm going to see you!"

And my father said, "Well, I know you've been coming to see your mama." He was anxious. Our triangle was a thin line now, its tensile strength unknown.

"Dad, I'm going to be here. Don't worry about it." In the meantime, I said, I'd be storing his cigarettes at the nurses' desk: "Mama's not here anymore to watch that you don't smoke in the room."

My father said, "Why can't you give them to me?"

"No, I can't do that."

"Why not?"

Which is how my father and I concluded that funereal, epochal day: arguing over his cigarettes.

The next day I was off to my *Eyewitness News* farewell party at Elaine's, my second home. They had booked the date months earlier, and I needed some distracting. My mother would have wanted me to go.

The party was an out-of-body experience. As I mingled with media and showbiz notables, cracking the requisite inside jokes, I felt as though I might float away. People sounded like they were underwater. I was told that the food was good that night, but I could not taste a thing.

Amid the banter and bonhomie, the fact that I'd lost my mother four days earlier was pushed into backstory. It was nothing I couldn't work around.

That would be my MO for some time to come.

TV news waits for no man, and it nudged me back to the front. Though my noncompete clause stalled my anchoring till June, I shot promotions a week after the funeral. We staged run-throughs with my prospective co-anchors. I was in and out of the office a dozen times that spring.

Even so, it was the longest sabbatical of my life. In the past, my house had served as a crash pad between assignments. With no wars or trials to divert me, it felt lonely and isolated. Like some O. Henry character, I found the time to reflect when reflection was too hard to bear.

My illusions died, I wrote in a sporadic journal. *I am no longer a child. I am a pip in an immense sea of indifference.* After my mother's death, I pushed away its enormity. When I felt thankful that her agony—and mine—were over, I had to close that door in a hurry. After my glimmer of open grieving in the limousine, I shut that door, too. My own reality seemed a tenuous thing. I slept but two or three hours a night; I clung to consciousness like a child shy of the inner dark.

Something stopped inside me when my mother died.

Denied its true expression, my grief breached in other forms: insomnia, jumpiness, galloping anxiety. When I sought catharsis in painting, my work screamed with livid reds, with figures crushed into corners of the canvas. My new job seemed a reckless gamble. I was being hailed, and handsomely paid, as the savior of the third-ranked station in a three-team race. The microscope would be out for me, and the knives as well. What if I were found wanting?

Looking back at them, my concerns were mostly irrational. The job would entail nothing that I had not done before. My real fear was of the unknown, of a life without my mother. I missed our three-a-day phone calls. *How are you feeling? What's Dad up to? How did you like the show?* There were times when I'd think, *I have to call Mom,* and catch myself reaching for the handset.

Through the spring, my days were what I made of them. Aside from the odd cameo at CBS, I had no obligations except for a cranky old man on Long Island. I would have kept tabs on my father in any case, promise or no. But I might have visited less often if not for the one who'd loved us both.

The irony was that my dad lent me structure when I sorely needed it. Weekday mornings (four or five per week when I could stand it), I would trek out to East Neck and arrive before lunch. I'd usually find him in the sunny smoking lounge, parked in his wheelchair before the TV. It was a pleasant room with large windows, beige linoleum, and soft yellow walls. There were low shelves packed with hardcovers and paperbacks; my mother had paged through quite a few of them, but I never saw my dad crack a book.

The furniture was Early Public School, all metal and wood with no upholstery—a good thing, or my father might have torched the place. Engrossed in a show, he'd forget his ashtray and scorch his shirts. Greedy for nicotine, he'd smoke his cigarettes down until he dropped the glowing butts in pain. Once he set his pajama bottoms on fire. I was fortunate to be there and put it out before any real damage was done.

If my father was out of sorts, he might stay the morning in his room. He received his ablutions from Mohammad, a wiry man in his forties who spoke little English—an ideal background for the task, as you could do your work in peace. The other aides were muscular women who'd loved my mother and took no guff. Each day my father was sponged head to toe. Every other day he was strapped into a harness and lowered into the tub, like a racehorse with a bowed tendon.

Hygiene was not my father's long suit. He'd dress himself and wind up a mess in day-old attire, soiled with the detritus of his drool and smoker's cough. He resisted the staff's intercession, especially if Mohammad was off. Only I could handle his midday "refreshers," a job to test my filial devotion. I checked my father's clothes and shamed him into changing: "Look at the stains on that sweater!" I replaced the torn and worn-out, kept his dresser well stocked. I maintained a fresh supply of berets.

If he needed it, I'd clip his nails and trim the hair in his ears. I moisturized his hands with the special lotion my mother used, working the leathery, yellowed fingers. I did things for my father I would not do for myself.

I fought off revulsion in most of these chores, but foot care was the worst. When I checked his gnarled feet, I saw death around the corner. The soles were craggy and ashen, the toenails warped like rotting seashells. I'd get over lots of things with my father, but it was hard to get used to his feet.

He responded with his native grace and gratitude. "Hey, you're hurting me!" he'd yowl as I wiped his face. "You've got heavy hands, just like your mother. You got to be gentle!"

Nevertheless, I did the job. I did it for my father to

keep his dignity. I did it so John Johnson Sr. would not look like a bum.

Once the patient passed scrutiny, I took him down to the dining room, to his old corner table. Oh, man, did I hate lunchtime. We'd start by hassling over the menu. Would he order a cheese sandwich (his favorite) or a hot meal with vegetables? Would he drink his coffee at the start (and kill his appetite) or wait till the end of the meal? When it came to food, my father was used to living in the tall grass. He missed my mother's collard greens and salt pork, her tasty fried chicken. The dull and healthy fare at East Neck left him cold.

I tried to move things along by cutting his meat, fetching his beverage. I would sit and fidget and say to myself, *How long can it take to pick up a sandwich and put it in your mouth and take a bite and chew?* In my father's case, it took roughly the half-life of strontium 90. The minutes crawled. Without my mother to emcee, we had little to talk about.

When he was done at last, I'd wipe his mouth and pushed him to the lounge, where we'd often be alone. The first order of business was to light his Carlton. When my mother was alive, I occasionally bummed one of my father's cigarettes, a small communion. But I'd quit cold turkey when she died, and now his smoke was killing me. Judging from his phlegmy cough, it wasn't doing him much good, either.

We spent the next hours in front of the soaps. My father preferred the bad girls, the Susan Lucci types, the mean ones with décolletage. As he got excited, he'd mumble back to the set: *Uh-huh!* He'd be glued to the pathos and bathos, smoking his brains out or munching on the Mounds bar I'd furnished, as my mother had before me.

Every once in a while I'd look up from my *New York Times* and muse, *How can he watch this crap?* Or I'd catch myself staring at the screen—lost in space, since the Byzantine plots escaped me—and think, *What am I doing?* I knew I was in trouble when I caught myself humming the theme for *The Young and the Restless.*

As much as I hated soap operas, they were handy as anesthesia and safer than conversation, especially when thoughts strayed to the Absent One. At a commercial break my father might say, "I sure do miss your mom."

And I'd say, "I know you do. I miss Mama, too, you know."

And he'd say, "I think of her every day." We'd start welling up, and I'd break down and ask him for a cigarette. I'd tell him not to cry, too late. Then I'd get incensed. Who was he kidding? I'd think back to my mother's deathbed and his pathetic requiem; I'd think of how he'd wronged her all those years. And I'd think, *If you miss her so much, why weren't you better to her in life?*

I guess you could say I wasn't ready to bond. Even had I been able to let go the past and overlook my father's misdeeds, there was a crime in progress that I could not absolve.

He had survived her. My mother was gone, and he was still alive.

I had always assumed that my father, three years older, would go first. He was the one who chain-smoked and melted into his recliner. But in the end, he carried the day. Lazy and self-absorbed, he was also self-sufficient and tough as nails. He'd outlasted Uncle Syl and Mama Tutt and my mother, and judging from how poorly Aunt Marian was faring, he would soon outlast her, too.

I was rough on my father in those first months on our own. I got on him about finishing lunch, or changing his shirt, or snuffing the damn cigarette before it singed his fingers. Why couldn't he try harder? Why couldn't he do better?

When he wearied of my brickbats, my father would

groan and say, "Oh, you're just like your mom!" (Hadn't I once heard a similar charge, in reverse?) He didn't have it quite right, however. I wasn't *like* my mother; I *was* my mother. I stepped into her shoes without missing a beat. I was my dad's eagle-eyed monitor, his boon companion, his harshest critic.

Though I didn't see it at the time, I must have hurt him. He would say, "Your mother sure did love you." When I'd answer that she loved him as well, he'd insist, "Oh, no, you favor your mom, and your mom sure did love you."

I'd check my watch as it crawled toward three o'clock, when I'd bail out to beat the traffic. After my father went to rest, I burst out of the lobby like a kid on the last day of school: *Hallelujah!*

Feeling high on fresh air, I jumped into the Ferrari and jacked up the stereo and spun away, leaving death in my rearview mirror.

On June 5, 1995, I reported for my first official day at WCBS. My office was crammed with so many bouquets that I could barely squeeze inside. I'd either made the big time, I thought, or just crashed my own funeral.

My station promoted me daily. My face was plastered across billboards and on city buses, captioned by our new slogan: "New York to the Bone!" No need to append my name. Didn't everyone in this town know Big John Johnson?

The hoopla was enough to turn a person's head, if not inflate it like the Goodyear Blimp. But while I relished my perks, my complimentary airline upgrades, I stayed wary of fame. I had seen the rampant self-love of too many anchors. They were Ted Knight personified: pompous, petty caricatures. You knew they were gone when they rushed home to watch themselves on tape. I refused to do it, because that was the Jonestown grape juice. It would kill your real life.

As soon grew apparent, WCBS *was* a funeral for most everyone involved. Our news director was an erratic ego-maniac, the "talent" a bevy of back-stabbers. In the space of one week, the two candidates for co-anchor each invaded my office, trashed her rival, and collapsed in tears.

None of this was extraordinary in our business. The difference was that I had lost my sounding board. I could no longer ring my mother and say, *Do you know what these people are doing?* There was no one to tell me, *Oh, Johnny, don't worry about those other people. You just go ahead and do your work—you're doing great!* Once I could deflect the nonsense, on-camera and off. Now I took it home with me.

I felt like a college frosh all over again, the one who'd ascended against all odds. I'd spent most of my life frantically getting here, which was far more motivational than being here. The title and money were nice, but what exactly was the point? My mother was my engine, my compass, the person I most wanted to please. Without her to share the glory, I ran out of steam. By the time I got the anchor job, I didn't really want it.

And so I became the creature I'd scorned: another passive, pleasant face reading the TelePrompTer, distinguished only by my deeper tan. Twice each day, I went on the air with a grin and a quip for the weatherman, and no one could have guessed at how hollow I felt.

Or that I had taken a bullet to the brain.

Even at half-speed, my job left little spare time. But I couldn't write off my father. Barring trips out of town, I still went to East Neck at least twice a week. I'd take off for the Island by nine and stay till one, then head back for my ten-hour shift. I plunged into the maw of the evil morning rush hour, where it might take two hours to make the sixty-five miles. But I was determined to keep my weekends free and salvage what was left of my sanity.

It's hard to pinpoint exactly when it changed between my father and me. I think it began at one of a thousand lunches where he balked at eating his drab vegetables. I was about to play my broken record: *Come on, Dad, you've got to eat your string beans, they're good for you.* But for some reason I flashed back to a Gates Avenue morning . . .

"You're a growing boy and you need the protein," my father said, cracking two raw eggs into a half-pint of milk. He eyed me sternly as I took the glass. Halfway through I started gagging, but I knew that I could not stop. He wouldn't let up until I drank it to the bottom . . .

Even as a ten-year-old, I knew that the egg milk was less about nutrition than my father's need for control. And now—shame on me—I was running the same scam. I put on great shows of solicitude at the nursing home. Conscious of observers, I made clear that I was prodding Dad for his own good.

In fact, I was getting my payback. I was berating him as my mother had, out of anger, end of story.

As epiphanies go, that was a big one. I had no quarrel with the old man sulkily picking at his green beans. My fight was with a fiend who dwelt in my dark corners, a composite of buried resentments. I suddenly saw my father for what he was now: an octogenarian with a broken-down body, a mild case of dementia, and little incentive to change his ways. How could I be angry with *him?* Life was cruel enough already; I didn't need to make it worse.

From that point forward, I lightened up. Rather than ride my father to stop smoking, I made sure that he wore his body-length plastic apron. Instead of mocking his soap operas, I pulled my nose out of the *Times* and joined the party, with dialogue out of *Beavis & Butthead.*

Well, Dad, how do you like her? Do you think she's pretty?

Oh yeah, I like that, ha-ha-ha . . .

One day, after we rolled onto the elevator to go to lunch, I noticed an administrator, a staid woman in her forties, standing as far away as she could. As we disembarked, she said to me, "Mr. Johnson, you're going to have to do something about your father. Nobody's safe in the elevator with him. I can't get on without him trying to touch me!"

And my father retorted, "Oh, that's not true. That's not true!"

It was true, of course. My father had been goosing women at East Neck ever since he got there. "Inappropriate behavior toward aides," his social worker wrote. "Touching them in a sexual manner and making lewd remarks." When my mother was alive, my father's trick was to wait till a nurse came to take her temperature, then reach through the curtain and grab the woman's bottom. (My mother would smack his hand and remind him, "I'm here, John, don't you do this while I'm here!")

Now he used me as bait, calling out, "You know my son? Come on over here and meet him!" As his target steered a wide berth, he'd tell me, *sotto voce*: "That's what I'm talkin' about. Look at her butt!"

Once he surprised me with a proposal to marry a woman down the hall. I said, "Are you crazy? Why would you want to do that?"

"Well," my father said, with soft-shoe timing, "I really just need a room and an hour, you know."

My dad's libido was tricky for me. I felt shamed by his rudeness. I hated it when he pumped for details of my own social life: *You getting some?* I remembered when the dirty old man wasn't so old, when he kept a mistress and harassed my college girlfriends.

At the same time, I felt heartened that he had a pulse. There were days when my father was lost in confusion or the blues, barely stirring in his chair. Then a woman approached, and it was like an elixir; he'd perk up and shed twenty years. But as she passed, his body slumped. His eyes filmed over; he slipped back into his death fog. For all his bravado, he was no longer a player and he knew it.

I kept a watchful eye on Aunt Marian the day of my mother's funeral. She let nothing out, which was her way. I remembered the time she called me to get Fatty to the doctor. She'd sensed that my mother wasn't feeling well that day, out of the blue, and she was right. As we filed out after the casket, I said to myself, *She is not going to be able to survive this.*

After losing her mother and ex-husband, the death of her sister was a lethal blow to my dear aunt. She told her daughter, "I feel like a part of me has died." Sickly and depressed, she moved in with Dianne in South Jersey. She was hospitalized in September 1995 with what would be tardily diagnosed as ovarian cancer.

When I visited over the next months, she'd retell the old stories of how Fatty had saved her from the neighborhood toughs. They had a unique bond, too strong for even my father to subvert.

The last time I saw Aunt Marian, I brought a teddy bear to the hospital. When I said goodbye and looked back at her, she was clutching my gift like a little girl. She died later that week, almost a year to the day after her twin. My mother's family was gone, those wonderful people, the salt of the earth. I would never meet their like for magnanimity, or fortitude, or simple, innocent joy.

We buried Aunt Marian in the Bronx, next to Mama Tutt. It was, I thought, the last piece of my mother going under ground.

"Let's make a little history," the news director had said in wooing me to WCBS. It was the best mash line since the walrus and carpenter lured the oysters to dinner.

In television, however, history is a short-term affair.

Our ratings were low as I debuted and did not improve. There were rumbles from Westinghouse, our new parent company. The news director was fired. A month later, less than a year and a half after being hyped as "the quintessential New York journalist," I was called into the big office. I'd just signed off the five o'clock show: *I'm John Johnson, Michele and I will be back at eleven* . . .

"I want you to clear out your desk," said the general manager, a corporate type known for his surly temper and over-the-paunch slacks. "You're not doing the eleven o'clock show."

Stunned, I asked him, "Who's taking my place?"

"Don't worry about that. It just didn't work out—I'm sorry, okay? One more thing, you better leave by the back way. Somebody leaked this to the press."

I was bewildered; I had never been fired before. I didn't feel any better to learn that they'd guillotined six other anchors and reporters, the biggest bloodbath in New York TV history.

I picked up my umbrella. I walked out the front door and issued my terse "no comment" to the microphones and cameras. (My co-anchor wasn't quite so composed. "No, no, no!" she wailed, before running back into the building.)

The next morning I got a call from Dennis Swanson, an old friend and the general manager of WNBC. Five days after that, I was hired for the noon anchor slot with a four-year contract worth more than $2 million. I moved to Rockefeller Center, into the old RCA Building, where my father once washed the floors.

WNBC treated me well, and I will be ever grateful for their rescue. But the change of venue failed to salve my misgivings about our business. In our lust for ratings, we were all dumbing down with a vengeance. Publicists drove the morning meetings. If the "visual" was good enough—say, a stockbroker in a Donald Duck suit—we'd shoot the promo before doing the reporting.

A decade earlier, I might have had the brass and energy to shake up the formula. Now I took shortcuts like the rest. When I got my hefty paycheck, I felt like I was stealing. When I glimpsed my face on the JumboTron in Times Square, I saw a swollen fraud. In *La Dolce Vita,* Marcello Mastroianni plays a tabloid reporter who knows that his work is worthless, but feels powerless to change. That was me. In the middle of my show, as we cut to commercials after some vapid "human interest" story, I'd find myself laughing out loud on the set. People must have thought I was a lunatic.

I needed time and solace to absorb my mother's death, and I'd allowed myself neither. The penalty would be substantial. In battening my doors against bereavement, I shut out other feelings as well. My relationships flat-lined; friends drifted away. I even stepped back from my children.

Senses dulled, I sleepwalked through my daily routine. *Drive down Palisades Parkway and across George Washington Bridge . . . park in 50th Street garage . . . walk block and a half to office . . . pass crowds waiting for free tickets to Conan O'Brien . . . up employees' elevator to fourth floor . . . down hall to makeup room . . . get fluffed by hair stylist . . . go out and do news . . .*

No one of these activities held any more interest than the rest. I had lost . . . *feeling.* It was something like your arm or leg going to sleep, except for me it was my soul.

CHAPTER FOURTEEN

THE DAY I DECIDED TO QUIT MY JOB, I WENT TO DENNIS SWANSON and said, "I can't do this anymore." I didn't want a leave of absence. I didn't care to bet that the cancer would kill my father as projected, or to bargain for more time if he lingered. I desired no favors, no strings, just a graceful farewell.

I agreed to take the week to think things through, but I'd already cleaned out my office. To achieve what I was after, I needed to leave my old life behind.

The decision wasn't so difficult once I'd made it, not for me, anyway. My accountants were horrified. My agent was flabbergasted. By opting out in the first year of my deal, I was leaving millions on the table. Was I insane?

When I ran into Harry Belafonte, whom I'd known for years, he said, "You're a black man who's *out* there. You're in a position to help the cause." (Had he been watching me lately?)

And I said, "No, it's over. I've got to hang out with my father."

And Harry said, "You are one dumb Negro."

When I saw the columnist Cindy Adams, she said,

"What were you thinking to quit this job? What kind of a schmuck are you?"

I was the happiest kind. I felt a little insecure that week, but I enjoyed a great sense of freedom. I'm reminded of Socrates's didactic: *What are you doing?* You can say that you're shopping at the mall, or going to Vegas for the weekend, or anchoring a news show, but *what are you doing?* I'd tailored my life for praise and acceptance, but I quit my job for me. I somehow trusted that there would be life after television, that I might even be a better man without it. For the first time in a long while, I knew what I was doing.

I was sure of myself . . . until I broke the news to my father in the smoking lounge. I said, "You're going to be seeing a whole lot more of me, Dad. I quit my job so I can be with you."

I'm not sure what I expected, but it wasn't what I got. He looked puzzled and said, "What about the money?"

I said, "You mean my salary? Well, I think I have enough put away."

And he said, "You're not going to be on television anymore?"

"No," I said, "I'm going to be here with you."

My father said not another word. He sat in his chair and puffed and coughed and stared up at his soap opera. *Was he disappointed?* I had a chilling thought: He preferred watching me on television to seeing me in the flesh. He couldn't care less about my quest for self-knowledge. He cared about his bragging rights with the nurses: *That's my son on Channel 4!*

Quietly, I panicked. What had I been thinking? Had I really aborted my career to attend this impossible man? I had a vision of my father dribbling applesauce out of his mouth while I squirmed in discomfort, one *Groundhog Day* after the next. I felt like the biggest fool in the world.

But as the minutes passed and we sat wordlessly together, I saw a smile play at my father's face. The news sank in. Whatever lay in store for him, he would not be facing it alone.

On August 8, 1997, my mother's seventy-ninth birthday, I signed off my show as usual: "I'm John Johnson, good news to you."

The man in the mural watched me exit one last time. I walked out of Rockefeller Center and drove to East Neck, swapping my vast tri-state viewership for an audience of one.

He was getting weaker now. Often he was sleeping when I got there, and I'd sit by his side till he awoke. I was back to five days a week, five hours per day; as my father could do less, I did more. I combed his hair and wiped the spittle from his mustache. I spoon-fed his spinach and mashed potatoes, waiting patiently for each swallow. I willingly massaged his feet. I even got used to the way he smelled.

When I was a little boy, I hated my father's odor. It was stale and smoky, nothing like my mother's sweet scent. When I came home in the afternoon and his smell was strongest, before he showered for work, I wriggled out of his hugs with a furrowed face.

But now his smell didn't bother me; it was a nice enough aroma, after all. As I became kinder to my father, my perceptions shifted. The sensory cues were the same, but they triggered different feelings.

On mornings when he was up and around, I might greet him with our old salute: a flurry of shadow punches and a light headlock. If he looked droopy, I'd steer the conversation to our mutual passion. Joe Louis, Sandy Saddler, Archie Moore, Sugar Ray Robinson—we'd swap stories about the titans, replay their best bouts. It felt good to have my father passing on what he knew again. It reminded me of what it meant to be his son. He was larger than his pathology. He had taught me things, too.

Despite some chinks in his memory, my dad could recover many a dim and dusty event. When I probed about our days in Washington, he replied that it was "a no-good town. You had that big old hole in your head, and the ambulance wouldn't come to the colored section, so I had to save your life." Never shy about taking credit, my father was definitely proud of that.

He recounted other tales, like the one about my first street scrap: "Remember when your mother wouldn't let you in the house? That Sonny chased you home, but he didn't bother you after that. Oh, you beat that Sonny."

Or: "Do you remember your Uncle Manzie? He was something. Lots of women and liquor, you know, but he could really play the drums."

Or: "Remember when I taught you how to drive? What was the first thing I taught you to do?"

Ever the eager student, I chanted, "To move into first on a hill and start off without sliding back."

"That's right!"

I was touched when my father recalled our trip to Radio City. I was delighted when he laughed, for the first time in months, at my account of the ROTC jacket, "when Ma thought I was off to the front." When he was feeling garrulous, and the weather was nice, I might switch off the soaps and wheel him out to the courtyard. My father wouldn't argue. He wanted to keep me happy; he wanted me to stay.

We couldn't talk for long without getting to Irene. About the time she fainted at the news of Dianne's first baby. Or how game she was to dance when I showed her the latest steps from Studio 54. "You looked pretty good in there against Floyd Patterson," my father said one afternoon, his preface to a pet anecdote. "What a night!

Your mother was there . . ." A pensive pause. "I sure do miss your mother . . . Could you light me a cigarette?"

Just as I'd treated my mom to her spritzers, I became the enabler with my dad. I'd light him one Carlton after another, till the air in the lounge turned blue. His cough was like a prelude to the grave. It squeezed his body into a knot before releasing him to puff again and seize up once more.

It was hard to watch, but my father didn't seem to mind, and the damage was already done. Smoking was his last sensual comfort. If it shaved another week or two off his life, that was his choice.

It was time to let the man be.

The month we'd been promised stretched to three, then four, then five. Gradually, without noticing, I'd lost all discomfort with my dad. I renewed an affection I'd thought had shriveled and died.

Once I checked in on him and pulled up short. Tilted to one side in his wheelchair, my father looked mordantly crooked and frail. Was this my curse, my nemesis—this sick old man with the baseball cap perched off-center on his head? When I sat next to him, his face creased into a smile: "Johnny Boy!" *The simple pleasures,* I thought. Some days it was hard for him to talk, and that was okay, too. I would stay as he sagged into sleep and left me to my thoughts. I stopped watching the clock. I was no longer on deadline.

When we moved through the corridors or into the dining room, he introduced me to anyone in our path: "Have you met my son? Do you know John Johnson? This is my son, John Johnson!" Five minutes later we might encounter the same person, and he'd start from the beginning: "He's my son, John Johnson!"

When we were alone, he might say, apropos of nothing in particular, "You sure are something!" Often he'd profess to be baffled: "I don't understand how you did what you did. Mm, mm, *mm*. How did you get to be you? I just don't know where you came from. Must have got it all from your mother, I guess." At that he would chuckle, but his self-effacement was real. My father thought he'd given nothing to my success. The spark was my mother's; all credit belonged to her.

The mystery cut both ways. As I delved into my father's life with an open heart, I couldn't imagine how he'd managed what *he* had done. How could he come home and feel good about cleaning a statue? How did he rise each day without despair?

By the time he left high school, my father's access to the good life was next to nil. As a teenager he had his mother to support, and soon after a wife and child. He had a few jobs he liked—the cab was "the most fun," he told me, "because you got to meet some interesting people"—and more that he did not. But he left his home each morning and found meaning in drudge work, because it was useful. It was needed. My father never won a Nobel Prize, but he mopped the floors and sorted the mail and put food on his family's table. Yes, he busted his hump. He *did* try, poor Jackie, and he'd never gotten credit for his efforts, least of all from his hostile son.

In its advanced stages, lung cancer can bring pain with every breath. There came a day when my father touched me for a cigarette and gasped for oxygen at the first puff. That was the end of his smoking, when he could physically stand it no longer.

As the disease took and took from him like some pillaging army, my father presided with remarkable calm. Once I asked him if he was scared of dying. No, he said, he wasn't afraid, and I believed him.

I won't pretend that we found our gauzy Hallmark moment. I wasn't spending Tuesdays with Morrie, or with Grandpa Walton; I could not blot away the brutal past. To my dismay, my father was still capable of soiling his wife's memory. "I had a girlfriend before I met Irene, you know," he told me one afternoon. "Her name was Hazel, and boy, I really liked her. I probably should have married her, but I took pity on your mother."

I forgot none of this, but I forgave it all. Dropping my grudge, my barricade, I saw my father as he was. I judged him in the light of his own needs and hurts instead of my own. I saw a man who had nothing until he had my mother, that vivacious, dynamic, extraordinary woman. She was the vessel for all that was inside him—for his ardor, to be sure, but also his frustration and self-loathing. Then a son came along, a mortal threat, because I could pirate away my mother's love. He knew that; he punished me for that.

The better I understood my dad, the less opaque I became to myself. In hating him, my conflict had tainted everything. I kept a running tally of my failures: the botched marriages, the missed chances. No relationship could fill me for long. No day could be perfect.

But as my father's life wound down, and I stopped parsing for flaws, I could view our lives through a clear, clean lens. Whatever our imperfections, I decided, we had each done the best we could.

That winter and spring, I spent some very good days at the nursing home, richly satisfying days—in their own way, almost perfect. Each time I learned something more, and there was so much I needed to learn. One morning I asked my father, "What kind of a little boy was I?"

He said, "You were the nicest, nicest little boy, and handsome, too. You were the smartest child I'd ever seen; I always knew you'd go to college. I'd tell people you started talking when you were nine months old, and they'd laugh, but it was true. And you were never any trouble."

I said, "Then why did I get so many spankings?" (Was that my voice quavering?)

He said, "I didn't give you many spankings, only when you needed it, like when you lied."

After all those years, his denial still nettled me. I was too fearful to lie as a child, and what did I have to lie about in the first place? But that was my father's story and he would stick to it. The truth—the grim history of his belt and heavy hand—was too threatening, especially now.

He would not repent, even at death's door.

In March 1998, more than six months after they found the cancer, my father began taking his meals in the day room by the nurses' station. This was the last roundup, where the patients sat slumped and half-napping, their wheelchairs stacked by a TV no one watched. The first time I saw him there, limp and slack-mouthed, I knew the end was near.

He was changing as infants change, day by day before my eyes. His skin lost its mahogany hue and stretched tight over his head, like a sheet of dull parchment. His face got thinner, his nose and ears larger. He was looking less like the man I knew and more like everyone else in that penultimate room.

My father still perked up, though, when I came through the door. I'd get him some applesauce and exhort him to eat. He'd try a few swallows, before giving up. When he coughed to clear his lungs, it was more a drawn-out wheeze. The effort taxed him, swung his head closer to his table, until he hovered within inches of his tray. I'd say, "Come on, Dad, try to lift your head up," and he'd work to please me.

As his stamina ebbed, our conversations narrowed. He began asking more about his grandchildren, and marveled that Eric had two sons of his own. He inquired about my latest girlfriend, whom he'd blur with women from years past. He didn't like me living alone. Would I give marriage another try?

"I don't know, Dad."

And he said, so softly that I had to strain to hear him, "You know, you need to be with somebody. You need to have somebody there for you." He was speaking from the heart. He missed my mother terribly, to the end.

I remember the last time we laughed together, when I told one of his favorite yarns: "Do you remember when we tried to fix the water faucet on Gates Avenue?" I was in the seventh grade, and my father was sick of the drip in the kitchen sink. Mr. Fixit attacked with a screwdriver, but the sink fought back. A flume shot out of the faucet. There was water everywhere, and my father shouted, "Do something!"

I plugged my finger into the hole, just like the little Dutch boy, but with somewhat less success. The water sprayed our faces. We stood there, sopping wet, because we couldn't stop howling.

Nearly fifty years later, we were howling still. "Why didn't you do something?" my father said, after catching his breath.

"Me?" I said, playing along. "I was just a little kid!"

Before I left that day, my father asked me, "You don't miss being on TV?"

I was candid: "No, I don't miss it at all."

That spring I took a room in a roadside motel to ease my commute. By mid-April my father could not keep down his food. His yellow eyes turned glassy and lifeless. He was fading clear away, and still he grinned his welcome each time I came by. In life he'd been grumpy as a matter of principle, the curmudgeon's curmudgeon. In dying he was tranquil as a lamb.

On Monday, April 20, I sat at my father's bedside most of the day, watching him struggle to breathe with his eyes closed. His lungs gurgled and tripped like a clogged carburetor, then popped clear for one more gulp of air.

He was drowning in slow motion, strangling by inches. I leaned over him, absorbed by the awful drama.

Suddenly my father's eyelids snapped open, like twin shutters wound too tight. He made a mighty effort to lift himself on his elbows and rise from the crypt. His face was dead except for his blazing eyes.

He looked straight through me and said, "Did you say goodbye to your father?" His voice was sharper than it had a right to be.

As I gaped at him, he repeated his piercing question— no, his demand: "Did you say goodbye to your father?"

Flustered, I replied, "Dad, you *are* my father."

I could tell he was displeased. He thrust his face closer to mine: "No, no, *no! Did you say goodbye to your father?*"

I flinched, as if warding off a slap. I tasted fear in an old, familiar way. I could hear my mother pleading, *No, Jackie, don't hit him, he's a good boy!* I felt clammy and intimidated. I had better answer, or else.

"Yes," I said. "Yes, yes! I said goodbye to my father."

As I mouthed the words, his body relaxed back into the bed. I touched his cheek and his breathing grew more even. When the nurse came by for his vital signs, she suggested I take a break. Nothing seemed to be imminent. Exhausted, I kissed my father on his forehead and left for a nap.

The phone was ringing as I entered my motel room. It was Sharon, the nurse. "You need to get back here *now*," she said.

He was gone by the time I got there, but I was all right with that. We had parted in character: he, the daunting parent, one last time; I, the placating child.

The good boy. The father's only son.

I sat by his bedside for what I'm told was half an hour. I can remember none of it. When I emerged from the room, dizzy and half-blind, Sharon took me by the arm and said, "I have something you need to know." She'd been with him as he died. According to Sharon, these were his last words:

Tell my son how much I love him, and how proud I am of him.

The line was so perfect that at first I thought she must have made it up. But the more I considered it, the truer it felt. My father *was* proud of me. Over the past eight months something had healed between us. Our rancor fell away like an old chrysalis, and a new kinship was born: of respect, and admiration, and love.

I'd asked for a closed casket, but someone garbled my instructions. The lid was open and I saw what I did not want to see: a waxwork of my father. The features were composed, the eyes discreetly closed, but the face was as distant as my mother's three years earlier.

While they closed the lid, I waited in the corridor and listened to Duke Ellington. I had chosen my father's favorite tunes, the reedy, big-band music he once danced to at the Renaissance Ballroom: "Sophisticated Lady"; "Mood Indigo"; "In a Sentimental Mood." The sounds put me closer to him in this anonymous, suburban mortuary.

At my mom's funeral, I'd made it through my eulogy without stopping. At my dad's I was shaky from the start. I bought time by looking out over the smallish crowd. Most of the guests had never met the man in the brown casket; they had come because of who he was to me. Once that might have seemed ironic. Now I was touched by their gesture.

I saw Eric, my firstborn, the grandchild who'd known my father best, crying soulfully. Though I ached to cry myself, I had to make my public parting. For some reason I began it this way:

"My father had beautiful hands. Elegant hands. The hands of someone who could have been *someone*." My own hands were shaking, and I took a beat to blink back my tears.

"But my father came and went in such an ordinary passage. He grew up as a black man in a terrible time to be a black man, and some part of him died as a result of that. He was hurt early on, left without a father at a young age. He had to make his way from his teens. Maybe someone else could have done it better, but I think that you have to walk in a man's shoes before you judge him.

"His whole life was a struggle, but he had one great gift, something to hold on to nearly all of his life: the undying love of my mother. And that made him more fortunate than most. He had a lot of wonderfulness in his life.

"My father was a person who believed that if you spared the rod, you spoiled the child. He believed in that to a fault and beyond. But he did as well as he could with me. My father did his job, and I think I did mine, too."

I could go no further. In a sense, my father's eulogy was also my own. It was the death of any chance to explain or be explained to. It was the end of the pair who bore me and raised me and drove me and loved me.

I'd been wrong to think that we'd buried the last of Fatty with her sister. Like it or not, my father was *the* central relationship of my mother's life. Now that her other half had died, she was truly gone. Two headstones stood on the family plot, side by side beneath a vaulting evergreen. A disconsolate orphan stood between them.

As I laid down the final rose on my father's casket, with my hands so much like his, a woman behind me started wailing. It was such a doleful, eerie sound. As I shut my eyes, I could almost hear my mother crying . . . crying for her man gone now.

Epilogue

AFTER MY MOTHER DIED, I KNEW THAT I COULD NEVER BE SO HURT again. With my father it would be different—once I made it through the funeral, the worst was surely over. My dad's death wasn't tragic in the same way. He had lived to a ripe age, and we'd had time to set things right. I could accept his passing without guilt or second guesses.

My burden lifted, I looked forward to resuming my life, all the painting and doing I'd deferred for eight months. Freedom beckoned; I had only myself to serve. I felt impatient to turn the page and get to the easy part of the book.

But a funny thing happened on my way to fulfillment: My wheels fell off. At night I'd revisit my old plummeting nightmares. Or I'd see myself encased in a stainless steel cylinder, temperature-controlled and vacuum-packed.

In other words, as good as dead.

My paintings went nowhere. I gained fifty pounds in a year. I was classically depressed.

In response, I did the things that modern troubled people do. I began to see a therapist. I took sleeping pills for my insomnia and, for a while, an antidepressant. I felt a little better, some of the time. But when I thought of my parents, I could scarcely breathe. My loss was like the great stones once used to crush the chests of heretics.

Now I can see I was not free at all. I carried my parents with me—the one's insecurity, the other's rage. I encapsulated my father's death. I locked it next to my mother's, in emotional storage, the old survivor's trick. I did everything but grieve.

And so I drifted through limbo until destiny interceded, in the form of Katie Couric. The story of my quitting television to care for my dad had spurred a few articles, then an interview on the *Today* show. Someone noticed. When a Rockland County hospice opened a bereavement counseling center five minutes from my house, I was invited as the keynote speaker.

On a sun-drenched, shirtsleeve day in September, more than three hundred people gathered on the lawn by the new building. There were tents for food and an a cappella chorus. Local pols made their canned remarks.

When I stepped to the dais, I don't recall being nervous. I'd been asked to deliver five minutes, a cakewalk. I began, "You are never prepared for death. Who expects their loved one to die, their parents to die?" As I moved to the meat of my speech, I inserted a personal anecdote—a stock rhetorical device, nothing more.

"My mother and father had known each other since they were thirteen and sixteen, when they met while roller-skating—"

That's where I faltered, at *roller-skating.* That's when I succumbed to the rush of images, flipping behind my retinas like the frames of a silent movie. My parents skating down Edgecombe Avenue in their first flirtation . . . dancing in Harlem's hottest ballrooms, cheek to cheek . . . matching strides as they raced along the beach . . . fussing over a doomed hand of bid whist. I saw them in Washington and Harlem, in Bedford-Stuyvesant

and Long Island, in their prime and their wasting ill-
nesses.

My parents, in the fullness of their lives.

Now they were finished, forever gone. The feelings I'd
caged through five years and two eulogies burst through
the links. My throat thickened, my eyes welled. I could
feel the water clinging to the rims of my lids. If I tried
one more word, I knew I would spill over—the heaving
shoulders, the works.

A stillness hijacked the up till now happy occasion.
The chitchat by the food tent muted; people froze in
mid-fork. They were joining in my sorrow, which made it
worse. I looked over the rows of rapt, white Republicans,
and I said to myself, *You do not want to do this. Do not
lose it here!* But there was nothing I could do. I was
about to fall down and roll on the ground, and the
county executive would be trawling me into the hospice
for bereavement counseling like no one had ever seen.

My paralysis lasted a full minute, an eternity for an ex-
anchorman. *Don't just stand there like a stump! Hum a
few bars! Do something!*

I cleared my throat and gripped tight the lectern. I
took a breath and began again: "My parents knew each
other since they were thirteen and sixteen—"

This time I couldn't get to the roller-skating. *Oh God,
not again! Please don't let it happen again!* I longed to
tell what it had cost me to manage my parents' lives and
deaths, and how essential it was to find support. But I
wasn't going to make it. Any moment now, the center's
director would materialize and wrap the cane around my
neck: *Let's thank Mr. Johnson for being with us
today . . .*

For another interminable lag, the only sound was the
gentle breeze. I finally choked out, "This is an important
event . . . and an important place. Anything I can do to
assist this hospice, I will do. I thank you very much."

I sat down, my body shaking. Applause rolled over the crowd and seemed to last a long time. As I made my get-away to the parking lot, people approached me in tears. A man told me, "We shared a memorial for your parents today, and it was very special. I want to thank you for it." A woman held my arm and kept repeating, "I know, I've been through it, I know just how you feel . . ."

Over the years I'd made hundreds of speeches, full of clever jokes and quicksilver transitions. But the one that worked best was barely verbal at all. Only when narrative failed me could I express what I felt.

I passed through a crucible on that suburban lawn. I hadn't intended to expose myself before all those strangers, but there you go. At home, whenever a wind-storm blew, I could turn on the TV or have a drink or take a pill. But swirling over me in public, in the warm light of an autumn afternoon, it was inexorable, and I was blown away.

Once the unbuttoning began, I could not stop. I came to understand why I fought my mother's death to the end, even after she herself had accepted it.

If I could keep her alive, you see, my fantasies could live as well.

My mother and father and I were bound in close and inextricable ways, too close for me to see clearly. While all children hold illusions about their parents, mine amounted to a full-blown, Freudian fiction.

To summarize: I had to slay my demon father to save my saintly mother and myself.

I believed that everything good in me came from my mom. She was the one who read me *Moby-Dick* and taught me to draw, who cheered and prodded me onto a bigger stage. She underwrote my life. By giving me the strength to overcome, she guaranteed I would not fail.

My father? He was my cross to bear, the source of all

pain and frustration. I was loath to give him credit of any kind. Even at the end, when I made my peace with the man, it was for my salvation more than his.

I'd never stopped fearing that I was my father's son. I didn't batter wives or children, but there are subtler forms of abuse. As I wrote upon my mother's death, in a florid scrawl of Magic Marker:

I hate my father. My father made me who I am!

By serving my time at the nursing home, I'd hoped to find that we were not the same. If I were ever to be sure that the devil wasn't in me, I needed first to look him in the eye.

It was only when we reconciled, and in the cool light after my father's death, that I saw his sway in its complexity. Yes, he'd been a force to push against, to toughen me for a tough world. But my father was more than a sadistic drill sergeant. In our time together at East Neck, I rediscovered the man who'd taught me to box and to drive, who braced my confidence when I needed it most. At his best, he'd made a scrawny youth feel competent in the world.

My dreams were dreamable, in part, because my father made me secure. Whatever his warts (and they were whoppers), he came home each day from work, steady as the sun. Drawing from his own dashed hopes, he pressed me to do more and try harder. When your father tells you a thousand times that you are going to college, no matter what, it inflates your sense of the possible. It forever alters your self-image to the good.

André Watts, the great pianist and a close friend, once told me, "It would be better not to have a parent than to have someone brutal."

As a case in point, I disagreed. I was the son of an alcoholic and a sexual predator, yet their message came through: I was to be something! I didn't become a mugger or a drug addict. Some good things must have happened in our household, and my dad was a part of them, too.

A shifting tide rocks all boats. Once I beheld my father as a man, instead of a malevolent stick figure, other revelations followed. I realized that our strife had served a purpose. For years it obscured an even more hurtful conflict:

The one I had with my mother.

Irene Tutt Johnson was a rare and marvelous woman, but hardly a saint. Along with her drinking and depression, her bent toward self-destruction, she was a practiced manipulator. Needing a buffer from her husband, she positioned me in the crossfire. In her weakness she sought protection that no little boy could provide. When I tried nonetheless, I judged myself wanting. It was my fault she got hurt, my failing, my flaw.

Worse, my mother used me to get back at my father. We colluded to exclude him from our clique of two, and my dad knew it. He was the odd man out—less sensitive, less cultured, less valued. While his vicious "discipline" was inexcusable, I began to see what had made him so angry.

Here was my mother's greatest sin: to set me against the essential man in my life. Our alliance was built on soft sand. By maligning her husband, then scolding me as his replica, my mother shredded my ego. I felt guilty for hating my father; I felt guilty for *being* my father.

Coerced to take sides, I stopped trusting either parent. I held only in myself, corroding my ties to come. How could I keep a wife when I could not trust her love, when I felt worthless of love in the first place? In a sense, the first woman in my life undermined the rest.

In demythologizing my mother, I did not blame the dead. I knew better than anyone that Fatty had lived under siege. Once I lighted her down from her pedestal, where the air was too thin and the view too misty, I might have loved her even more.

Maybe it took my parents' dying for me to love them as they were.

I made my mother's Brunswick stew a time or two after she died. It tasted wrong, and the memories were too sad, so I stopped.

Over the past four years, I've moved gingerly to thinking of my parents in the past tense. My mother is dead and I cannot save her. My father is dead and I cannot even our score. I must shelve my regrets alongside my mom's recipes; I am sixty-three years old and I have no days to waste.

While I remain a work in progress, the progress is plain. I am a healthier person than when my father died. Working five days a week with a sparring partner, I've shed the fifty pounds. I confine my drinking to an odd glass of champagne. I'm sleeping better, without pharmaceutical aid. I'm more tolerant and forgiving, even of myself.

I still need to take more chances, to give more to both love and art. But whatever I choose, it will be for me, not my parents. I no longer need their Greek chorus of approval. (*Was it okay?* I'd ask at the end of each show.) My challenge is simply to do, without worrying what people think. It's the difference between a camera and a canvas. The one pulls your energies outward; the other forces you inward, to face yourself.

After my memorable appearance at the hospice, I knew that I'd done right to quit television. I had to slow down to stop running from life; I had to shear the nonessentials to find what mattered. My semi-solitary stretch at East Neck freed me to a simpler existence. I have less excitement these days, and it's to my liking. It seems that I just might be content.

And when I think of my parents, my pain and anger have dissolved. I am left with a success story: of a couple who stayed together, whatever their problems. They built a home and put poverty behind them. They doted on their child and gave him what he needed to prevail.

They did their job and I did mine, too, and who is to say that it wasn't good enough?

Acknowledgments

THIS MEMOIR HAS LED A CHARMED LIFE OF ITS OWN. PATTY MARX, a wonderful writer and humorist, was the first person to suggest that my story might be a book. She introduced me to the publishing world—and in particular to Deb Futter, then vice president at Random House, who made an initial offer and helped me find an agent, the estimable Esther Newberg. Beyond her fabulous skills as a negotiator, which led to a better deal with Time Warner, Esther was astute enough to recognize that I could not write this book on my own. She connected me with Jeff Coplon, my simpatico co-writer, and it was then that this project became real.

I was truly fortunate when our editor, Jamie Raab, came into my life. Jamie believed in this book from the beginning, and supported it with patience, insight, and unfailing sensitivity. She kept us on course with a kind and creative hand.

Sharon Burns is one of those people who go about making others' lives better every day, too often without thanks or recognition. As a nurse at East Neck Nursing and Rehabilitation Center, she did so much for my parents in their final years, and saw to it that they passed on without pain. She was a huge support for their only son.

I owe a debt of gratitude to Dominick Sclafani, the East Neck administrator, and to his entire staff, for the care my parents received there. Dominick also provided detailed medical reports that proved invaluable to this accounting.

Dianne Wood, my dearest relative, was a vital source of information about our family tree, and in particular about our unforgettable grandmother, Mama Tutt. While I'm proud that she is my first cousin, I've always thought of her as my little sister.

Over the years, Ana Maria Braga has served as my assistant, my researcher, and my producer. As my closest associate, her heroic work ethic was instrumental to my rise as a newsman. Yet more important, Ana was the surrogate daughter my mother never had, a surrogate parent to my children when I was on assignment, and my selfless friend. Without Ana's detailed notes and work logs, spanning twenty years of my life as a journalist, this book would have been far more difficult to write. I owe her more than I can say.

I must mention two old friends: Sandy Pearl, who told me I could not be whole until I came to terms with what my parents meant to me, and André Watts, who was wise enough to say, "Go and paint, John"—to know that I needed to change my life.

Finally, I want to thank Ann Yih for supporting my decision to leave television, for offering a shoulder when my dad died, and for discovering the title of this book.